THE WAR TO END ALL WARS

THE WAR TO END ALL WARS

WORLD WAR I

—✦— BY —✦—

Russell Freedman

sandpiper

Houghton Mifflin Harcourt

Boston • *New York*

Frontispiece: A German soldier helps British wounded make their way
to a first-aid station during the Battle of the Somme, July 1916.

The poem "Lost in France" by Ernest Rhys is reprinted
here with the kind permission of Stephen Rhys.

The text of this book is set in 13-point Sabon.

The Library of Congress has cataloged the hardcover edition as follows:
Freedman, Russell.
The war to end all wars: World War I / by Russell Freedman.
p. cm.
1. World War, 1914–1918—Juvenile literature. I. Title.
D522.7.F74 2010
940.3—dc22
2009028971

ISBN: 978-0-547-02686-2 hardcover
ISBN: 978-0-544-02171-6 paperback

Manufactured in China
SCP 15 14 13 12 11 10 9

4500828103

In memory of my father, Louis Nathan Freedman,
who served with the U.S. Seventh Infantry Division
in Alsace-Lorraine, France, 1918

*There were great numbers of young men who had never been in a war
and were consequently far from unwilling to join in this one.*

—THUCYDIDES, FIFTH CENTURY B.C.

CONTENTS

THE GREAT WAR

Those who lived through World War I called it the Great War because of its massive scale: some two dozen countries joined the conflict, which swept across continents and killed perhaps 20 million people.

This was the first full-scale war in which modern weapons inflicted mass slaughter. Long-range artillery, rapid-fire machine guns, poison gas, flamethrowers, tanks, and airplanes that bombed and strafed introduced new kinds of terror and record levels of suffering and death. It was the bloodiest conflict the world had ever seen. The survivors sought comfort in the belief that this terrible war surely would be the last. By the time the exhausted combatants finally laid down their arms, the Great War was also known as the War to End All Wars. Of course, it wasn't known as World War I until the outbreak of a second world war in 1939.

Mighty empires collapsed as a result of the fighting. New nations came into being. And the war's aftershocks are still being felt today. The Russian Revolution, the rise of Hitler, America's emergence as a world power, the Second World War, and continuing turmoil in the Middle East all have their roots in the First World War. More than that, this war changed forever the way wars are fought and the way people think about the use of military power.

World War I inspired a flood of poems, novels, memoirs, songs, plays, and films that attempted to capture the horrors of modern warfare and the anguish and grief that follow in its wake. David Lloyd George, a future prime minister of Great Britain, said at the time that if the war could just once be described in honest and accurate language, people everywhere would demand that the fighting be stopped.

Canadian stretcher-bearers bring in a wounded soldier.

Lost in France

He had the ploughman's strength
in the grasp of his hand;
he could see a crow
three miles away,
and the trout beneath the stone.
He could hear the green oats growing,
and the southwest wind making rain.
He could hear the wheel upon the hill
when it left the level road.
He could make a gate, and dig a pit,
and plough as straight as stone can fall.
And he is dead.

—ERNEST RHYS (1924)

Archduke Franz Ferdinand and his wife, Sophie, set out in their motorcade in Sarajevo on the morning of the assassination, June 28, 1914.

1

MURDER
IN SARAJEVO

It was a perfect day for a parade. Crowds lined the parade route, waiting to catch a glimpse of Archduke Franz Ferdinand, heir to the imperial throne of Austria-Hungary, seat of the thousand-year-old Hapsburg Empire. Smiling expansively and nodding to the crowd, the archduke was riding in an open car through the streets of Sarajevo on the fateful Sunday morning of June 28, 1914. Sophie, his wife, sat beside him, wearing a broad-brimmed hat to shield her cheerful, plump face from the summer sun.

Franz Ferdinand had brushed aside warnings that his visit was unwelcome and that his presence in Sarajevo might in fact be dangerous. Sarajevo was the capital of Bosnia, a rebellious province recently annexed by Austria-Hungary, usually referred to simply as Austria. The people of Bosnia included a large number of Serbs, who resented being ruled by foreigners. They wanted to free Bosnia from Austrian domination and make the province part of the independent Kingdom of Serbia, their own national state.

Scattered among the crowds that morning were six young terrorists. Five of them were teenagers, university students of Serbian descent who had been born and raised in Bosnia. All were members of a revolutionary organization called Young Bosnia. They had been recruited, trained, and armed by the Black Hand, a secret group dedicated to the expansion of the Kingdom of Serbia and the liberation of all Serbs living under foreign rule. Their mission was to strike a blow against Austria and the Hapsburg monarchy by assassinating Archduke Franz Ferdinand. Their battle cry was "Death to the tyrant!"

As the terrorists waited in the crowd, events were spinning crazily out of control. The leader of the Black Hand, known by the code name Apis, had masterminded the assassination plot. Now he was having second thoughts. An assassination, he feared, might lead to war between little Serbia and its powerful neighbor Austria. Apis dispatched a message to the terrorists, ordering them to abandon their plan. But it was too late. The assassins were dead set on moving forward. One of them would later tell an interviewer that in going to Sarajevo "he only wanted to die for his ideals."

And while the terrorists did not know it, the man they intended to kill was actually sympathetic to their cause. Franz Ferdinand was to eventually inherit the Hapsburg crown from his eighty-three-year-old uncle, Emperor Franz Joseph, and he planned to give the Bosnian Serbs a greater voice in the Austro-Hungarian government.

As the imperial motorcade drove toward Sarajevo City Hall, one of the terrorists hurled a small bomb at Franz Ferdinand's passing car. The bomb landed in the street and exploded against the next

car in the procession, spraying shrapnel and injuring two officers on the archduke's staff. After the would-be assassin was captured and the injured men were taken to a hospital, Franz Ferdinand insisted on continuing to City Hall, where he was greeted by the mayor. "So you welcome your guests here with bombs?" the archduke remarked with some anger.

At the formal welcoming ceremony, the mayor delivered his prepared speech as though nothing unusual had happened. Franz Ferdinand then asked to be driven to the hospital so he could visit the two wounded officers. He wanted his wife to stay safely behind, but Sophie insisted on accompanying him. The governor of Bosnia had assured the royal couple that the police were fully in

After being greeted by the mayor, Franz Ferdinand and Sophie descend the steps of Sarajevo City Hall to their waiting motorcar, a few minutes before they are shot.

control. There would be no further trouble, he promised. The terrorists would not dare to strike twice in one day.

And so the imperial motorcade set forth again. On the way to the hospital, the archduke's driver took a wrong turn. Realizing his mistake, he stopped the car, shifted gears, and prepared to turn around. By chance, the leader of the terrorist gang, nineteen-year-old Gavrilo Princip, happened to be standing on the pavement a few feet away. Princip had melted unnoticed into the crowd after his accomplice had thrown the bomb. Now he saw his chance. He stepped forward, pulled out his revolver, pointed it at the archduke's car, and fired twice.

At first it appeared that no one had been hurt. Franz Ferdinand and Sophie remained calm and upright in their seats. But as their car sped away, blood began to spurt out of Franz Ferdinand's mouth.

"For heaven's sake!" Sophie cried. "What's happened to you?" Then she slumped forward, her head falling into her husband's lap.

"Sophie, dear. Sophie, dear, don't die!" Franz Ferdinand pleaded. "Stay alive for our children!" Members of his staff crowded frantically around him, pulling open his coat, trying to see where he had been shot. "It's nothing," he gasped. "It's nothing."

Sophie died almost instantly. The bullet that killed her had passed through the door of the car, striking her in the groin and severing an artery. The archduke, shot in the neck, bled to death within a few minutes.

Gavrilo Princip, the teenage assassin, tried to shoot himself in the head but was overwhelmed by members of the crowd. As he struggled, he managed to swallow a vial of cyanide, a deadly poison that each member of the gang was carrying. But the cyanide was old and only made him vomit. He was arrested on the spot. Later, in prison, he expressed his regret at Sophie's death. He had not meant to shoot her.

Above: The assassin, at right, is hauled away by the police.

Right: Nineteen-year-old Gavrilo Princip. He died of tuberculosis in his prison cell four years after the assassination.

Two of Princip's accomplices had also been captured. They confessed that they had been armed in Serbia and smuggled across the Austrian border with the help of Serbian border guards.

Austria had long regarded the Serbian kingdom on its borders as a threat. The Serbs had won their independence in 1878, after centuries of resistance to Turkish rule. They had greatly expanded their territory and population during the Balkan Wars of 1912 and 1913. The Serbian government was dedicated to the idea of a "Greater Serbia" and to the liberation of all Serbs living under foreign rule.

The assassination of Franz Ferdinand convinced high-ranking Austrian officials that a war was necessary to curb Serbia's

EUROPE BEFORE THE WAR

ambitions. Serbia "must be eliminated as a power factor in the Balkans," warned Count Leopold von Berchtold, the Austro-Hungarian foreign minister. Berchtold predicted a swift Austrian victory over Serbia, with no wider repercussions.

"The Serbs must be disposed of, and that right soon!" declared Kaiser Wilhelm II, emperor of Germany, Austria's closest ally. Other European leaders were not so sure. They feared that an Austrian war against Serbia might set off a deadly chain reaction, pulling in other nations, such as Serbia's ally, Russia.

Europe's Great Powers, as they called themselves, considered their options and began to eye one another warily. Several crises in the recent past had been resolved peacefully by diplomacy. A peaceful resolution was the hope of Sir Arthur Nicholson of the British Foreign Office. "The tragedy which has just taken place in Sarajevo," he wrote, "will not, I trust, lead to further complications."

The crowned heads of Europe—some of whom would soon be at war—assembled in 1910 for the funeral of British king Edward VII. Edward's son and successor, George V, is seated at center. Standing behind him is his cousin Kaiser Wilhelm II of Germany. Albert, king of the Belgians, stands next to the kaiser, on his right.

2

ARMED TO THE TEETH

European powers had been fighting one another for centuries, but as the summer of 1914 began, Europe was at peace. Alfred Nobel, the Swedish inventor of dynamite and founder of the Nobel Peace Prize, had predicted that his powerful explosives might very well put an end to all war. Rather than annihilate one another, the nations of Europe would have to settle future disputes through negotiation and compromise.

Close economic ties among European countries also made a major war seem unlikely. Prosperity depended on international trade and cooperation.

In addition, there were blood ties linking Europe's royal houses. Kaiser Wilhelm II of Germany and King George V of Great Britain, grandsons of Britain's Queen Victoria, were cousins. Czar Nicholas II of Russia was a cousin by marriage: His wife, Alexandra, was one of Victoria's granddaughters. Another granddaughter, Ena, was queen of Spain. Except for France and Switzerland, every nation in Europe was a monarchy, and almost every European head of state was related to every other.

Most Europeans looked forward to a peaceful future. "The world is moving away from military ideals," declared the influential British journal *Review of Reviews,* "and a period of peace, industry, and world-wide friendship is dawning." It was easy enough to ignore the rivalries and suspicions among Europe's great powers that spelled trouble ahead.

Germany was an ambitious young nation. The German states had become a united country only in 1871, as a result of victorious wars against Austria and France. By 1914, the German Empire, with its dynamic economy and industrial might, had emerged as the most powerful nation on the continent of Europe. Germany was competing with its neighbors for trade, influence, and colonies overseas.

Great Britain and France, the leading colonial powers, ruled much of the world beyond Europe's shores. They each possessed a far-flung network of overseas colonies, a source of immense wealth and national pride. Germany, a latecomer to the race for overseas possessions, had only a few colonies in Africa and the Pacific. Striving to be recognized as a world power as well as a European power, Germany sought to extend its influence in the few remaining areas of the world that were not under European rule.

The Germans already had a big army, equipped with the latest weapons. To compete for colonies, Germany's leaders decided that they also needed a modern oceangoing navy that could challenge Britain's centuries-old command of the seas. German shipyards

rushed to build a fleet powerful enough to engage Britain's Royal Navy in battle.

Britain relied on its navy to safeguard the trade routes that brought riches to the small, densely populated British Isles and helped feed the British people. Germany's ambitions were seen as a threat to Britain's naval dominance. British leaders responded by launching an ambitious shipbuilding program of their own. So along with a rivalry to grab overseas colonies, Britain and Germany engaged in a costly competition to build bigger and better battleships.

If Britain felt challenged by Germany's aggressive push to become a world power, Germany felt threatened by France and Russia, its neighbors to the west and east. The French had suffered a humiliating defeat in their war with Germany in 1870–71, when France was forced to surrender the provinces of Alsace and Lorraine, a loss that France could neither forgive nor forget. Fear and resentment of Germany had drawn France into a military

German battleships steam into the North Sea. Germany's race to build a powerful navy was seen as a threat to Britain's command of the seas.

alliance with Russia, which also looked upon the newly powerful German Empire on its border as a threat.

Germany's chief ally was Austria-Hungary, an unwieldy empire of several major religions and numerous languages and nationalities, including large numbers of Serbs who wanted to break away from the Austro-Hungarian Empire and declare their independence. The Serbs, like the Russians, were among the Slavic-speaking peoples of eastern Europe. They looked to Russia for protection and support. Austria-Hungary, determined to hold its rickety empire together, suspected Russia of deliberately encouraging unrest.

Rivalries among Europe's Great Powers had led to an elaborate network of military alliances, in which one nation pledged to support another in the event of war. Germany and Austria-Hungry had joined with Italy in what was called the Triple Alliance. France and Russia had an alliance of their own. And Britain, while avoiding formal alliances, had signed ententes (understandings) with both France and Russia, forming what was known as the Triple Entente.

As the European nations chose up sides, they were busily arming themselves. Military leaders warned that it was essential to be

Russian troops parade in honor of French president Raymond Poincaré during his state visit to Russia, July 1914.

strong and prepared, as a warning to any aggressor. So along with the naval armaments race between Britain and Germany, European nations were competing in an arms race on land. Seeking security in military superiority, they recruited ever larger armies and navies, piled up more and more of the latest new weapons, and built wider and stronger fortifications along their national borders.

This arms buildup alarmed some observers. Czar Nicholas II warned that "the accelerating arms race" was "transforming the armed peace into a crushing burden that weighs on all nations and, if prolonged, will lead to the very cataclysm it seeks to avert."

On June 28, 1914, the day that Archduke Franz Ferdinand was assassinated, the major European powers all had large standing armies. And they were all armed to the teeth.

The assassination triggered a diplomatic crisis. Austria blamed the government of Serbia for the royal murders and for constantly stirring up trouble. Austrian foreign minister Berchtold called for a "final and fundamental reckoning with Serbia."

Austria issued an ultimatum—a list of demands—that, if accepted, would compromise Serbia's independence. The Austrians knew that an attack on Serbia might draw in Russia, Serbia's champion. So before delivering the ultimatum, Austria obtained a pledge of support from its ally, Germany, in the event of a war.

The Austrian ultimatum was delivered to the Serb capital, Belgrade, on July 23, 1914. When the Serbs refused to meet the Austrian demands, Austria declared war, confident of German support if the war spread.

On July 28, Austrian guns fired across the Danube River, at that time the boundary between the two countries, lobbing shells into nearby Belgrade and hitting a hospital. "Windows were shattered to smithereens," reported a Serbian doctor, "and broken glass

Kaiser Wilhelm directing the German army's 1906 maneuvers. He took great pride in his role as All Highest War Lord.

covered many floors. Patients started screaming. Some got out of their beds, pale and bewildered. Then there was another explosion, and another one, and then silence again. So, it was true! The war had started."

Austria now began to mobilize its armed forces, calling up hundreds of thousands of reserve troops and moving men into combat positions. Mobilization in any country was a lengthy process that could take weeks. Once the Austrians had assembled their troops, they planned to march into Serbia and settle the score by means of a swift offensive. Meanwhile, diplomats hurried back and forth between European capitals, exchanging notes, hoping to contain any fighting and avoid a wider conflict.

The Russians were not eager to intervene, but they could not simply abandon their fellow Slavs of Serbia. Russian generals persuaded Czar Nicholas to order a partial mobilization, in response to Austria's full-scale preparation for war. If Russia reacted quickly and forcefully, perhaps Austria would take note and hold back. The German ambassador to Russia warned that Russian mobilization would compel Germany to gather its troops in turn, "and that then a European war could scarcely be prevented."

Alarmed at the prospect of war, Czar Nicholas appealed directly to his cousin, Kaiser Wilhelm. "To try and avoid such a calamity as a European war," the czar telegraphed, "I beg you in the name of our old friendship to do what you can to stop your allies from going too far." The telegram was signed "Nicky."

Before he received the czar's telegram, the kaiser had sent the czar a telegram of his own, signed "Your very sincere and devoted friend and cousin, Willy." "I am exerting my utmost influence," he wrote, "to induce the Austrians to deal straightly to arrive [at] a satisfactory understanding with you."

But Austria was determined to punish Serbia. And by now, Germany had responded to Russia's move by ordering a partial mobilization of its own. When word of the German action reached the Russian capital, Czar Nicholas, after much hesitation, ordered the full mobilization of Russia's armed forces. "Think of the responsibility which you are asking me to take!" the czar told his foreign minister. "Think of the thousands and thousands of men who will be sent to their death!"

Austria's threats of war had set off an escalating chain reaction. As one country's mobilization led to another, the rush of events overwhelmed the ability of diplomats to resolve the crisis. From then on, military calculations rather than diplomacy guided decisions in every European capital. Europe's leaders began to act as though war were inevitable.

Mobilizing a nation's armed forces has been compared to drawing a gun. Theoretically, the nation that has its forces ready first gains a huge military advantage. An army that fails to take the offensive in time might be destroyed before it can complete its preparations.

With Russia preparing for war on its eastern border, Germany decided that it must order a full mobilization too—unless Russia halted its plans. The Germans now dispatched ultimatums to both Russia and its ally France, warning that "[German] mobilization will follow unless Russia suspends war measures against ourselves and Austria-Hungary." The ultimatum to France declared, "Mobilization inevitably means war," and demanded a guarantee of French neutrality.

On August 1, Britain's King George V telegraphed his cousin Czar Nicholas: "I cannot help thinking that some misunderstanding has produced this deadlock. I am most anxious not to miss any possibility of avoiding the terrible calamity which at present threatens the whole world."

But the king's message arrived too late. Earlier that evening, the German ambassador to Russia, Count Friedrich von Pourtales,

Czar Nicholas II and his future wife, Alexandra, a granddaughter of Queen Victoria. This was their official engagement photo.

requested a meeting with Russian foreign minister Sergei Sazonov. The two diplomats were old friends. Pourtales, visibly upset, asked Sazonov if Russia was prepared to answer the German ultimatum. Sazonov, as he recalled the meeting years later, replied that it was not possible to stop the Russian mobilization that was now under way. Even so, Russia wanted to continue negotiations and hoped to avoid a war.

"In that case, sir, I am instructed by my government to hand you this note," Pourtales said. He pulled a paper from his pocket and handed Sazonov a declaration stating that because of Russia's continued mobilization, a state of war now existed between Russia and Germany.

At this point, the German ambassador burst into tears, and Sazonov began to weep too. The men embraced, then pulled apart.

"This is a criminal act of yours," Sazonov told the German ambassador. "The curses of the nations will be upon you."

"We are defending our honor," the ambassador replied.

"Your honor was not involved," Sazonoff said. "You could have prevented the war by one word; you didn't want to."

Then Sazonov escorted the tearful German ambassador to the door. The two friends never saw each other again.

France, like Russia, rejected the German ultimatum and declared a general mobilization. On August 3, convinced that French forces were about to attack its western border, Germany declared war on France.

Germany had a secret military plan that would go into effect if the Germans faced a two-front war against France and Russia. German troops would immediately sweep through France, occupy Paris, and knock France out of action in the west before Russia had enough time to fully mobilize. Germany could then shift its forces to the east, avoiding a lengthy war on two fronts. The intricate German war plan called for the deployment of a million troops transported by 11,000 trains according to a precise timetable. Once set in motion, the plan could not be stopped without putting Germany at a crippling disadvantage.

The Germans had demanded free passage through neutral Belgium in order to attack France. When the Belgians refused, Germany declared war on Belgium. On August 4, 1914, German troops marched across the Belgian border. Britain had been watching events from across the English Channel, its critical sea route to

Cheered and saluted by a patriotic crowd, a German cavalry regiment parades through Berlin as it leaves for the war front, August 1914. Their traditional spiked headgear will soon be replaced by more practical steel helmets.

A woman marches alongside French
troops as they leave for the front,
August 1914.

the outside world, and now felt threatened. Britain declared war
on Germany, joining France and Russia. During the next few days,
Austria-Hungary declared war on Russia, while France and Britain
declared war on Austria-Hungary.

And so Europe was caught up in a war that few had expected

and almost no one wanted. Even today, historians continue to debate the tangled and confusing causes of the conflict, the series of accidents, blunders, and misunderstandings that swept the nations of Europe toward war in the summer of 1914, whether war might have been avoided, and which persons or nations were most responsible. Wars in the past had often been caused by countries seeking more land or natural resources, or acting out of suspicion and fear of their rivals. And once a country is fully armed and poised to attack, war, it seems, is hard to avoid.

The events that unfolded as Europe careened toward catastrophe appeared to defy logic and common sense. Austria had wanted to punish Serbia, and then, one by one, other nations were drawn into the quarrel. To support Austria in its conflict with Russia over Serbia, Germany had attacked France by invading Belgium. And Britain had declared a state of war throughout the vast British Empire. In the rush of events, the Kingdom of Serbia, supposedly the cause of the war, had almost been forgotten.

Each nation believed that it was fighting a defensive war forced upon it by someone else. And each army was convinced that it could defeat its enemies within a few months and that the troops would be home by Christmas.

German infantry troops advance across Belgium, August 1914.

3

TO BERLIN!
TO PARIS!

Six million soldiers were on the march across Europe during the first weeks of August 1914. German cavalry troops advancing at a steady trot had crossed the border into neutral Belgium. French troops had attacked German Alsace-Lorraine, confident that they could recover those two lost provinces. A British expeditionary force was about to sail across the English Channel and link up with French forces fighting in Belgium. In the east, Russian troops, poised on the border of East Prussia, were about to invade Germany and advance toward Berlin.

As the war began, France, Britain, Belgium, and Russia became known as the Allies. Germany and Austria-Hungary were called the Central Powers. Several European countries, watching and waiting on the sidelines, would soon choose sides. But others, including Switzerland, Holland, and Sweden, would remain neutral and play no part in the fighting.

Kaiser Wilhelm, confident of a German victory, assured his departing troops that they would be home "before the leaves have fallen from the trees." His soldiers looked forward to occupying Paris and marching in triumph down the Champs-Élysées. French troops were just as certain that they would march victoriously into Berlin and parade along that city's famous boulevard, Unter den Linden.

In the capital cities of all the combatant nations, the outbreak of war was greeted with emotional displays of patriotism. Crowds thronged the streets, singing their nation's songs and cheering every military unit that passed. In Paris, people were shouting, "To Berlin!" while in the German capital, crowds urged their army on to Paris.

"In the first days of mobilization there was of course a lot of

Crowds outside Buckingham Palace cheer King George, Queen Mary, and the Prince of Wales following the declaration of war.

British recruits at rifle drill during basic training, September 1914.

enthusiasm," recalled Robert Poustis, who was a French student at the time. "Everybody was shouting and wanted to go to the Front. The cars, the railway wagons loaded with soldiers were full of tricolor [French] flags and inscriptions: '*À Berlin, à Berlin.*' We wanted to go to Berlin immediately, with bayonets, swords and lances, running after the Germans. The war, we thought, was to last two months, maybe three months."

Swept up in an outpouring of patriotic fervor, young men flocked to recruiting stations all over Europe. In Britain alone, nearly a million volunteers had enlisted by the end of 1914. Fired up with the conviction that their cause was a noble one and the enemy an aggressor, they joined the colors and went to war.

As men left for the front, women took their places in the work-force. Women had traditionally worked in fields such as teaching and nursing. Now, in every warring nation, women took over jobs previously filled by men in munitions factories, offices, and

Hitched to the plow: French farmwomen at planting time. With men away at war, women across Europe took the men's places on farms and in factories and offices.

agriculture, and, as the war continued, in almost any sort of job that could free a man for combat.

"I'd never been in a factory before, but the crisis made you think," a British housewife, Mrs. M. Hall, remembered. "I thought well, my brothers and my friends are in France, so a friend and I thought to ourselves, well, let's do something. So we wrote to London and asked for war work. And we were directed to a munitions factory. . . .

"We worked ten hours a day, that's from eight in the morning . . . until half-past six. . . . It was a perfect factory to work in:

everybody seemed unaware of the [explosive] powder around them, unaware of any danger. Once or twice we heard, 'Oh, so and so's gone.' Perhaps she'd made a mistake and her eye was out, but there wasn't any big explosion during the three years I was there."

Most people supported their governments. To many Frenchmen, the war was a crusade to save justice and liberty. To many Germans, it was a struggle to save civilization.

Germany had a deeply rooted military tradition in which the army enjoyed great prestige and played a dominant role in the government. Kaiser Wilhelm, surrounded by his military entourage, always appeared in the medal-bedecked uniform of the "All Highest War Lord" at the constant parades and celebrations of past military victories.

When war was declared, the kaiser addressed the enormous crowd that had gathered beneath his palace balcony. "A fateful hour has fallen upon Germany," he announced. "Envious people on all sides are compelling us to resort to a just defense. The sword is being forced into our hands. . . . I command you all to go to church, kneel before God and pray to him to help our gallant army."

A young German soldier, Walter Limmer, joined the army with his brothers, because, as he told his parents in a letter home, "That is the simple duty of every one of us. And this feeling is universal among the soldiers, especially since the night when England's declaration of war was announced in the barracks. We none of us got to sleep until three o'clock in the morning, we were so full of excitement, fury, and enthusiasm. It is a joy to go to the Front with such comrades. We are bound to be victorious! Nothing else is possible in the face of such determination to win. My dear ones, be proud that you live in such times and in such a nation, and that you too have the privilege of sending several of those you love into this glorious struggle."

A British propaganda poster depicts a German nurse pouring a glass of water on the ground in front of a wounded British soldier pleading for a drink. Both governments issued propaganda accusing the enemy of horrific and usually imaginary atrocities.

On both sides, government propaganda painted the enemy in the darkest terms. Emotions ran high. When Britain declared war on Germany, an angry crowd gathered outside the British embassy in Berlin, shouting insults, hurling stones, and smashing windows. The next day, as the British ambassador and his staff prepared to leave, the embassy's three German employees, having been paid a month's salary in advance, stripped off their embassy uniforms, spit and trampled on them, and refused to help carry the ambassador's trunks down to the waiting taxis.

In the Russian capital, St. Petersburg (soon to be renamed Petrograd), an angry mob broke into the German embassy, smashing in a side door. "I could see flashlights and torches moving inside," an eyewitness reported, "flitting to the upper stories. A big window opened and spat a great portrait of the Kaiser at the crowd below. When it reached the cobblestones, there was just about enough left to start a good bonfire. A rosewood grand piano followed, exploded like a bomb; the moan of the broken strings vibrated in the air. . . . The bonfire was being fed by the furniture, books, pictures and papers which came hurtling through the windows of the Embassy."

Gruesome atrocity stories began to appear in the newspapers. The German public read that the invading Russians were poisoning German lakes and cutting off the limbs of captured German soldiers, and that the French and Belgians were gouging out prisoners' eyes. The French were told that the Germans bayoneted babies, raped children, and cut off the hands of French boys so they could never become soldiers. None of the stories were true, but people believed and repeated them. "However the world pretends to divide itself," declared the English writer Rudyard Kipling, "there are only two divisions in the world today—human beings and Germans."

Anti-German feelings in Britain ran so high that families with German names felt compelled to rename themselves. The royal family, for two centuries known as the House of Hanover (a German city), became the House of Windsor, still its official name today. German shepherd dogs in England were renamed Alsatians, and dachshunds (German for "badger dogs") were kept under wraps by their owners and rarely seen in public.

Almost everyone expected a short war and a glorious victory. German soldiers marched off with flowers in the muzzles of their rifles. "Our march to the [train] station was a gripping and uplifting experience," Walter Limmer told his parents.

Austrian soldiers wave cheerfully as they depart for war.

"Such enthusiasm!—the whole battalion with helmets and tunics decked with flowers—handkerchiefs waving untiringly—cheers on every side. . . . This hour is one such as seldom strikes in the life of a nation."

At the same time, a similar scene was taking place at a train station in Paris. "At six in the morning," a French officer reported, "without any signal, the train slowly steamed out of the station. At that moment, quite spontaneously, like a smoldering fire suddenly erupting into roaring flames, an immense clamor arose as the Marseillaise [the French national anthem] burst from a thousand throats. All the men were standing at the train's windows, waving their [caps]. . . . The crowds waved back. . . . Crowds gathered at every station, behind every barrier, and at every window along the road. Cries of '*Vive la France!*' '*Vive l'armée!*' could be heard everywhere, while people waved handkerchiefs and hats. The women were throwing kisses and heaped flowers on our convoy. The young men were shouting '*Au revoir! À bientôt!*'"

While soldiers on both sides went to war in a holiday-like atmosphere, their optimism wasn't universally shared. The British philosopher Bertrand Russell "discovered to my horror that average men and women were delighted at the prospect of war." A week after the fighting began, Russell wrote, "'Patriots' in all countries acclaim this brutal orgy as a noble determination to vindicate the right; reason and mercy are swept away in one great flood of hatred. . . . Whatever the outcome, [the war] must cause untold hardship and the loss of many thousands of our bravest and noblest citizens."

Russell greatly underestimated the carnage that the war was about to cause. In 1914, Europe's armies had only limited experience with the mass slaughter made possible by modern weapons.

Belgian troops defend a hastily assembled roadblock in the town of Alost. At bottom left, a Belgian soldier lies either wounded or dead. The position was abandoned shortly after this photo was taken, August 1914.

"THE MOST TERRIBLE AUGUST IN THE HISTORY OF THE WORLD"

Germany's war plan was to sweep across Belgium and invade France from the weakly defended north. German generals were convinced that the outnumbered Belgians would not put up a fight.

Before advancing through Belgium, the Germans had to attack and destroy the powerful network of forts around the city of Liège, just inside the Belgian border. On the first day of the invasion, in the first major battle of the war, the Germans, to their astonishment, met determined Belgian resistance. As German troops tried to cross the Meuse River and storm the defensive forts, the Belgians opened fire and drove them back.

Company after company of German soldiers assaulted the hilltop forts, only to be mowed down by machine-gun fire. At Fort Barchon, the attackers "came on line after line," a Belgian officer reported, "almost shoulder to shoulder, until as we shot them down the fallen were heaped on top of each other in an awful barricade of dead and wounded. . . . So high did the barricade become that we did not know whether to fire through it or to go out and clear openings with our hands. . . . But would you believe it?—this veritable wall of dead and dying enabled those wonderful Germans to creep closer, and actually to charge up the [hill]. They got no farther than halfway because our machine guns and rifles swept them back."

To demolish the forts, the Germans brought up giant howitzers, firing shells that smashed through steel and concrete. One after another, the Belgian forts were blasted into submission. When the last fort surrendered on August 17, the Germans began their march across Belgium, driving thousands of frightened refugees before them.

Rumors spread that the Belgians were planning a guerilla war of sabotage and assassination. Surprised by Belgian resistance and enraged by heavy German casualties, German soldiers imagined that snipers were shooting at them from every window and rooftop, even when there were no snipers in the area. In reprisal, German troops rounded up and shot hundreds of ordinary civilians, including women and children, and burned villages to the ground. At one place, a German officer reported, "the whole village was in flames, cattle bellowed desperately in barns, half-burned chickens rushed about demented, two men in peasant smocks lay dead against a wall."

"Our advance in Belgium is certainly brutal," German general Helmuth von Moltke admitted, "but we are fighting for our lives and all who get in the way must take the consequences."

At the university town of Louvain, known as "the Oxford of Belgium," nervous German soldiers misinterpreted a nighttime movement of their own troops. The Germans panicked. Shouting, "Snipers! Snipers!" they began to set fire to buildings where

Two women pick their way over rubble and debris outside the ruined town hall of Louvain, Belgium, September 1914.

suspected guerilla fighters might be hiding. During three days of chaos and looting, the university's priceless library of medieval books and manuscripts was burned, more than a thousand buildings were destroyed, 209 civilians were killed, and the rest of the population of some 40,000 was forcibly evacuated.

Eyewitness reports shocked the British and French public. Newspapers in both Europe and the United States called the German invasion "the rape of Belgium." Wildly exaggerated accounts of German atrocities inflamed public opinion and bolstered support for a war that was increasingly seen as a crusade against barbaric German militarism. German newspapers, in turn, carried

Refugees fleeing to Holland after the German bombing of Antwerp, Belgium.

equally exaggerated accounts of German soldiers being savagely mutilated and killed by Belgian townsfolk. Germany's propaganda minister would claim that German actions were justified by military necessity and by self-defense. But he admitted that events in Belgium had "aroused almost the entire world against Germany."

German troops continued their advance across Belgium, overwhelming the small Belgian army and marching victoriously through Brussels, the capital, on August 20, 1914. The Germans now were opposed by French forces that had moved northward to meet the German invasion and by a British expeditionary force that had crossed the English Channel and taken up positions to the west of the French. But the advancing Germans, backed by heavy artillery, could not be stopped.

Again and again, the Germans would dig in, wait to be attacked, and then mow down their attackers with rifle fire, machine guns, and artillery such as howitzers and cannon. As the attackers

"The Most Terrible
August in the
History of the World"

35

fell back, the Germans continued to pound them with their long-range field artillery.

During one futile counterattack, "the French infantry made a gallant show, advancing across the Belgian beet fields with colors unfurled and bugles sounding the shrill notes of the 'charge.' As the ranks drew near to the German lines . . . rifles and machine guns pounded forth a rapid-fire of death from behind walls and hummocks and the windows of houses. Before it the attack wilted. Running, stumbling, crawling, the French sought cover as best they could, and the attack ended leaving the German Guard the undisputed masters of the field."

"It is clear that all the courage in the world cannot prevail against gunfire," said a young French captain named Charles de Gaulle, who later became president of France. In a single day, August 22, the French lost 27,000 men, most of them shot dead by machine guns and long-range rifles or blown to bits by shrapnel and high explosives.

Falling back all along the line, the French and British armies were forced into a retreat that would take them to the outskirts of Paris. During the month of August, more than a hundred thousand soldiers—French, British, Belgian, and German—were killed on the Western Front; several hundred thousand were wounded. British author Arthur Conan Doyle, the creator of Sherlock Holmes, called it "the most terrible August in the history of the world."

The Great Retreat, as it came to be known, continued for two sweltering summer weeks at the end of August and the beginning of September. Day after day under a scorching sun, hundreds of thousands of weary French and British soldiers trudged farther and farther south, covering some twenty miles a day, pausing again and again to fight off the enemy snapping at their heels. Each infantryman lugged a ten-pound rifle and sixty or more pounds of ammunition, digging tools, and other equipment as he plodded along in stiff, mud-caked boots that inflamed heels, soles, and toes and rubbed whole patches of skin to the raw flesh. The columns of retreating troops stretched out along the roads for miles. Scores of stragglers dropped behind the retreating columns, hobbling alone or in twos or threes and struggling desperately to stay in touch with their units.

Cavalry troops dismounted and walked beside their horses, trying to conserve the weary animals' strength. Horses were important because they also pulled the big guns, the ammunition wagons, and the wheeled field kitchens that cooked on the march. They "soon began to droop their heads and wouldn't shake themselves like they normally did," British trooper Ben Clouting remembered. "They fell asleep standing up, their legs buckling. As they stumbled forward . . . they lost their balance completely, falling forward and taking the skin off their knees."

Behind the retreating armies—and sometimes beside them, in the spreading confusion of the mass retreat—marched hundreds of thousands of German soldiers as tired as their enemies. "Our soldiers are worn out," a German officer reported. "For days they have been marching forty kilometers [twenty-five miles] a day. The ground is difficult, the roads are torn up, trees felled, the fields pitted by shells like strainers. The soldiers stagger at every stop, their faces are plastered with dust, their uniforms are in rags. . . . They march with closed eyes, and sing in chorus to keep from falling asleep as they march."

German troops crossed the Marne River and approached Paris early in September. The French government fled the capital for the city of Bordeaux on the Atlantic coast. And the French army made plans to blow up the bridges across the Seine River in the center of Paris and to destroy the Eiffel Tower, which was being used as a transmitting station for French army radio communications.

The Germans advanced to within twenty-five miles of Paris but

Two heavily laden French infantrymen.

found themselves physically exhausted and far ahead of their supply lines. As they prepared to march on the capital, the German right flank separated from the rest of the invading force, opening a gap between the German First and Second armies—a gap that Allied troops began to penetrate. Recognizing the enemy's vulnerability, the Allies seized the opportunity to make a stand along the Marne. "Attack, whatever happens!" French general Ferdinand Foch commanded. "The Germans are at the extreme limit of their efforts. . . . Victory will come to the side that outlasts the other!"

More than one million men fought in what history calls the First Battle of the Marne, which raged for eight blood-soaked days in September. "The heat was suffocating," a French cavalryman remembered. "The exhausted troops, covered with a layer of black dust sticking to their sweat, looked like devils. The tired horses . . . had large open sores on their backs. The heat was burning, thirst intolerable."

At one point during the fighting, French general Joseph-Simon Gallieni commandeered 2,000 Paris taxicabs, which rushed

British troops cross a pontoon bridge over the Marne River during the First Battle of the Marne, September 1914.

THE WAR IN THE WEST

thousands of French reinforcements to the frontlines. Against all odds, it seemed, the battle turned the tide against the Germans, stopped their advance, saved Paris, and came to be known as "the Miracle of the Marne."

The Germans were as astounded as everyone else by the battle's outcome. "That men who have retreated for ten days, sleeping on the ground and half-dead with fatigue, should be able to take up their rifles and attack when the bugle sounds, is a thing upon which we never counted," said German general Alexander von Kluck. "It was a possibility not studied in our war academy."

On September 14, the Germans began an orderly retreat. Along a front of some 250 miles, German soldiers did an about-face and started to retrace their steps over ground won in bitter fighting during the previous two weeks. The entire German force fell back to defensive positions along the Aisne River, north of the Marne, as the French and British followed cautiously. When the Germans reached high ground behind the Aisne, they began to dig furiously, preparing fortified trenches that they would defend against Allied attacks for the next four years.

British troops march along a French road lined with poplar trees during the blazing summer of 1914.

During the First Battle of Ypres in October 1914, British troops load a quick-firing eighteen-pound field gun, the mainstay of the Royal Field Artillery in World War I.

— 5 —

STALEMATE

By the autumn of 1914, fighting on the Western Front—Belgium and France—had shifted back to the north as the opposing armies maneuvered to outflank one another. From their entrenchments along the Aisne River, the Germans had advanced northward toward the French ports of Dunkirk and Calais on the English Channel. They were stopped by British troops who had taken up positions in and around the ancient walled city of Ypres (also called Jepar) in Belgian Flanders.

The First Battle of Ypres (it would not be the last) was fought during five cold and rainy weeks in October and November as the Germans attempted to break through to the Channel. Soldiers dashed from village to woods, from house to house, settling into firefights, charging with bayonets, attacking and falling back as shrapnel and high explosives rained down on the battleground.

"Every day the fighting gets fiercer," wrote Paul Hub, a young German recruit, in a letter to his fiancée. "All around me, the most gruesome devastation. Dead and wounded soldiers, dead and dying animals, horse cadavers, burnt-out houses, dug-up fields, cars, clothes, weaponry—all this is scattered around me, a real mess. I didn't think war would be like this."

Some of the hurriedly created German units were made up largely of students with little training, many as young as sixteen. Enthusiastic volunteers, they had left their lecture halls and school benches to fight on the Western Front, inspired by surging feelings of patriotism and a longing for military glory. They were led into battle by almost equally inexperienced reserve sergeants and officers. British soldiers would recall these schoolboy recruits advancing arm in arm, wearing their fraternity caps, carrying flowers, and singing as they came. They were mowed down in their thousands by British rifles and machine guns in what became known in Germany as the *Kindermord bei Ypern*, literally "the Murder of the Children at Ypres."

Today, the bodies of more than 25,000 of those young warriors lie in a mass grave near Ypres. At the site is a sculpture of a mother and father kneeling in grief as they mourn their lost son. The massacre at Ypres brought home the awful truth that the conflict was becoming a disaster for both sides. The war would not be short and glorious, as so many had wished to believe. Victory was nowhere in sight for either side.

The fighting at Ypres continued until the last week of November, when rain turned to snow and the mud froze. Trenches hastily scratched out in the boggy soil of Flanders had become part of a continuous line of fortified trenches that stretched 475 miles from the English Channel to the Swiss Alps. All along the Western Front, the opposing armies had been digging in to secure the territory for which they had fought. Now they crouched in their trenches, watching each other across a narrow and empty no man's land.

From the winter of 1914 to the spring of 1918, the pattern of trenches would remain fixed, shifting a few hundred yards here and there, or at the most, during a great battle, moving a few miles.

By the end of 1914, after less than five months of combat, more than 600,000 soldiers on both sides had been killed on the Western Front. For some fighting units, the losses were almost total. When Scotland's Second Highland Light Infantry Battalion was finally taken out of action, only thirty men remained of the more than one thousand who had come to France at the start of the war.

The First Battle of Ypres marked the end of the mobile war—the war of movement—on the Western Front. Trench warfare had begun along a front that would remain essentially unchanged for four more terrible years.

By the autumn of 1914, the opposing armies faced each other from across a network of fortified trenches that stretched from the English Channel to the Swiss border. Early trenches, like the one being dug here in the boggy soil of Belgian Flanders, were primitive compared to elaborate later defenses.

Russian prisoners being guarded by German soldiers on the Eastern Front in the autumn of 1914.

Russia, with Europe's largest army, had pledged to aid France by attacking Germany from the east—creating the war's Eastern Front. In August, while German armies were marching through Belgium, Russian troops invaded the province of East Prussia, the historic birthplace of the German Empire.

The Russians penetrated deep into German territory. But their supply system quickly broke down, and uncoded Russian radio messages were intercepted by the Germans, who blocked the Russian advance. The four-day Battle of Tannenberg ended with a humiliating Russian defeat as the czar's troops threw down their weapons and ran for their lives. Within a month of launching their invasion of East Prussia, the Russians had been driven back across their own border, and three-quarters of the 400,000-man invading force had been killed, wounded, or captured.

"[The czar] trusted me," the despairing Russian commander, General Alexander Samsonov, told his officers following the defeat at Tannenberg. "How can I face him again after such a disaster?" Wandering alone into the woods where much of the fighting had taken place, Samsonov shot himself in the head. His body was recovered and buried at his family estate. Thousands of his soldiers who had been killed in the same forest remained undiscovered where they fell, and their bones lie in the tangled undergrowth to this day.

The Russians had better luck fighting Austria-Hungary. When an Austrian army moved north to invade Poland, at that time a part of Russia, the Austrians were met by overwhelming numbers of Russian troops and were driven back in disorder across their own border into Eastern Galicia, Austria-Hungary's largest province. By November, the Russians had advanced into the wilds of the Carpathian Mountains, where they laid siege to the key Austrian fortress of Przemysl, now in Poland.

Austria appealed to Germany for help, and for the first of what would be many times, the Germans rushed to the rescue of Emperor Franz Joseph's battered army. German troops invaded Poland from the west, engaging the Russians in a succession of fierce battles around the cities of Warsaw and Lódź. The Russians finally lost Lódź in December, but they could not be ousted from their entrenchments around Warsaw.

The Austrians, meanwhile, also were being mauled by their troublesome little neighbor Serbia. Beginning in November 1914, Austria repeatedly invaded Serbia. But the Serbs were tough, seasoned fighters, and each time they drove the Austrians back across their border. By the end of the year, Emperor Franz Joseph's army could no longer hold its own against either the Russians or the Serbs without the help of the Germans, who concluded that they were "shackled to a corpse."

People now were beginning to speak of a "world war." Japan had declared war on Germany in August 1914 and seized German possessions in the Pacific and China. In Africa, French and British troops invaded the German protectorate of Togoland, while German forces attacked the British colony of South Africa.

In October, Turkey entered the war on the side of the Central Powers, expanding the war to the Middle East (then often called the Near East), where the British were backing an Arab revolt

As troops from the British colony of India march past, a woman pins flowers on a soldier's tunic.

THE WAR IN THE EAST

against the rule of the Turkish Ottoman Empire. Troops from distant parts of the British Empire—from Canada, Newfoundland, and Australia and New Zealand, known as ANZAC (Australian and New Zealand Army Corps); from India, South Africa, and the British West Indies—were arriving to join the British forces on the Western Front, where troops from France's colonial empire in Africa were also fighting At sea, British and German warships clashed off the coast of South America. And a British battleship shelled and destroyed a Turkish fort guarding the Dardanelles, the narrow sea channel leading from the Mediterranean to the Black Sea and Russia beyond.

In Belgian Flanders, the scene of savage fighting since October, the year 1914 ended with a remarkable display of fellowship and goodwill. On Christmas morning near the ruins of Ypres, German troops in their trenches opposite the British began to sing carols and display bits of holiday evergreen. The British soldiers replied by singing in return. Gradually, unarmed soldiers from either side began to show themselves atop their trenches, and cautiously, one by one, then in groups, soldiers from both sides walked out into no man's land and exchanged gifts of food and cigarettes.

"I think I have seen one of the most extraordinary sights today that anyone has ever seen," Second Lieutenant Dougan Chater wrote to his mother from his trench on the Western Front. "About 10 o'clock this morning I was peeping over the parapet when I saw a German, waving his arms, and presently two of them got out of their trenches and some came towards ours. We were just going to fire on them when we saw they had no rifles so one of our men went out to meet them and in about two minutes the ground between the two lines of trenches was swarming with men and officers of both sides, shaking hands and wishing each other a happy Christmas."

Christmas 1914 brought a temporary lull in the fighting on the Western Front. This German snowman is equipped with a spiked helmet and a Mauser 98 rifle.

For the rest of the day, not a shot was fired, and similar scenes were repeated in a number of places along the front. The British commander, Sir John French, was not pleased. "I issued immediate orders to prevent any recurrence of such conduct," he wrote, "and called the local commanders to strict account." A general order was issued, directing that "such unwarlike activity must cease." It did not happen again.

On the march: Strung out along a country road, Canadian cavalry troops and their horses move slowly toward the front, November 1917.

6

THE TECHNOLOGY
OF DEATH AND DESTRUCTION

An army on the march during World War I, with its plodding foot soldiers, its cavalry troops, and its workhorses pulling guns and equipment, moved along at the same pace as the army of Napoleon or Julius Caesar or Alexander the Great. Although soldiers in 1914 trudged down dusty roads as soldiers always have, the battles they fought were unlike any battles ever fought before.

Foot soldiers in the past had fought with single-shot rifles that could not fire very straight or very far and with crude short-range cannon. The earliest repeating rifles appeared during the American Civil War. By the time World War I broke out, lethal new weapons gave the armies of 1914 a concentration of firepower unimaginable in any previous period of warfare. Political leaders would find that the technology of warfare had advanced more rapidly than the ability of generals to control it.

European armies now were equipped with the latest fast-loading, rapid-firing rifles, deadly accurate at a range of hundreds of yards. Field guns had a range of up to five miles and could fire twenty rounds a minute. Heavy artillery, moved to the front by rail and tractor and set up on reinforced beds, could demolish targets more than twenty-five miles away. Armies came under fire long before they could see the enemy.

Every attack by the infantry's foot soldiers was launched with the support of a massive artillery barrage directed against the enemy's frontline defenses. For the first time in warfare, artillery dominated the battlefield.

British gunners perfected the "creeping barrage"—an advancing curtain of artillery fire that moved across the battlefield just ahead of the attacking infantry, providing cover as the assault came within yards of the enemy positions. High-explosive shells

Heavy guns, like these eight-inch howitzers of Britain's Royal Garrison Artillery, dominated World War I battlefields.

rained down upon enemy troops in their trenches, along with smoke and gas bombs that blinded the enemy and spread poisonous fumes. During World War I more soldiers were killed by artillery fire than by any other weapon.

The best defense against an infantry assault was an entirely new weapon, the machine gun, invented by an American-born engineer named Hiram Maxim. A machine gun could fire up to six hundred bullets a minute and, with its water-cooled barrel, could continue to fire at that rate for hours. Batteries of machine guns firing point-blank at assaulting troops could turn an infantry attack into a mass suicide. The effectiveness of machine guns as defensive weapons kept both sides from achieving a breakthrough and helped prolong the deadlock of trench warfare that immobilized the Western Front.

Another new invention, as simple as it may seem, became essential to the defenses of both sides. Barbed wire had been developed by American ranchers to keep cattle from breaking through fences. On the Western Front, especially, trenches were protected by dense belts of barbed-wire entanglements strung between wooden posts or metal pickets. The wire had to be positioned far enough out in front of the trench to keep the enemy from sneaking up to within grenade-throwing distance. At night, patrols went out into no man's land to repair wire damaged by artillery fire, or to clear a path through the entanglements in advance of an infantry attack the next day.

Attempts to break the stalemate on the Western Front led the British to invent another new weapon: an armored, gun-equipped vehicle that crawled along on steel caterpillar tracks capable of crushing barbed wire and crossing trenches. The project to develop these vehicles was a closely guarded secret. British officials put out the word that the huge, strangely shaped objects, kept under wraps beneath tarpaulins, were special water carriers—mobile tanks. They became known simply as tanks.

Tanks first went into action in France in 1916. Early models, made by both the British and the French, were so clumsy and mechanically defective that they often broke down on the battlefield, became mired in mud, fell into ditches, or were destroyed by enemy fire.

"When the first tanks passed the first line [of defense], we thought we would be compelled to retreat towards Berlin," a German lieutenant recalled. "I remember one tank, by the name of Hyena, which advanced very far and suddenly stopped about 1,000 yards from my little dugout. Some of the boys soon discovered that they could stop the tanks by throwing a hand grenade into the manhole on the top. Once this was known, the boys realized that there was a blind spot—that the machine guns couldn't reach every point around the tank, and these points were very important in the defense.

The interior of a British tank factory. The British army pioneered the use of tanks during the Battle of the Somme in 1916.

"I was shocked and felt very sorry for those fellows in the tanks, because there was no escape for them. Once a man was on top of the tank it was doomed to failure, and the poor fellows were not able to escape. The fuel would start to burn and after an hour and a half or two hours we saw only burning tanks in front and behind us. Then the approaching troops behind the tanks still had to overcome the machine guns of our infantry."

By 1918, the last year of the war, Britain and France each had produced several hundred improved tanks, which were more maneuverable and reliable than the earlier models. The British Mark V tank, equipped with two small cannon and four machine guns, had a crew of eight. It moved at five miles an hour over level ground and could concentrate intense cannon and machine-gun fire against enemy positions. The Allies, after much trial and error, learned to use their tanks effectively in coordination with artillery barrages, infantry assaults, and—toward the end of the war—attacks by low-flying aircraft. Germany failed to match the Allies in tank development, producing just one model, the cumbersome A7V, manned by a crew of twelve, which appeared too late in the war to have any real impact.

Perhaps the most terrifying new weapon was poison gas, introduced by the Germans at the Second Battle of Ypres, then quickly turned against them by the Allies. On the afternoon of April 22, 1915, following a heavy artillery bombardment, French Algerian troops noticed a strange grayish green cloud drifting toward them from the German lines. As the cloud reached the French trenches, men began to clutch their throats, coughing and choking, turning blue in the face. Soon thousands of panicking French soldiers were streaming to the rear. Several thousand others, unable to move, lay sprawled on the ground, gasping for breath. Within an hour, the Allied troops had abandoned an eight-thousand-yard stretch of the frontline. The Germans, meanwhile, were so afraid of catching up with their drifting gas

British troops blinded by tear gas await treatment at a first-aid station, April 1918. Poison gas of various kinds, used by both sides, could blind, burn, and kill.

that they advanced only a couple of miles before they were stopped by Allied reinforcements.

This was the first effective use of poison gas in any war. The Germans had opened 6,000 pressurized cylinders containing a total of 160 tons of chlorine gas, which the afternoon breeze carried toward the French lines. Chlorine destroys the ability of the lungs to absorb oxygen, causing victims of the gas to suffocate.

From then on, poison gas in a variety of forms was used extensively by both sides. Phosgene, more deadly than chlorine, was also an asphyxiant—it too caused death by suffocation. Mustard gas burned and blistered the skin, caused temporary blindness, and, if inhaled, flooded the lungs and could lead to a lingering and painful death.

Poison gas caused a lot of misery, but as a weapon it never proved decisive in any battle. Its effectiveness was limited by shifting wind directions, and by the rapid development of protective gas masks. Even so, gas attacks killed, blinded, or disabled tens of thousands of soldiers.

A British officer caring for gas attack victims near Ypres one day reported that "quite 200 men passed through my hands . . . some died with me, others on the way down. . . . I had to argue with many of them as to whether they were dead or not." All together on that day, "90 men died from gas poisoning in the trenches; [and] of the 207 brought to the nearest [medical] stations, 46 died almost immediately and 12 after long suffering."

Following the war, most countries signed the Geneva Protocol, a treaty banning the use of poison gas and bacteriological (germ-spreading) weapons. Although such weapons were stockpiled by the major combatants during World War II, fear of retribution kept them from being used in any significant way.

Flamethrowers were another terrifying weapon that had only limited effectiveness. Two tanks were strapped to the operator's back. Pressurized gas in one tank was used to propel a flaming jet

Protective gas masks for soldiers and horses were introduced soon after the first gas attacks.

of oil from the second tank as far as forty yards. While the flamethrower was frightening, it was almost useless when employed at a distance against fortified trenches. And it was dangerous for the operator. If a bullet penetrated both tanks strapped to his back, he would be engulfed in flames, spraying fire in all directions as he twisted and turned in the agony of death.

Aviation was still a novelty when the war began. The Wright brothers had made their first flight at Kitty Hawk in 1903, less than eleven years earlier, and by 1914 airplanes were still simple and few. But they quickly proved their value.

At first, aircraft were used mainly to carry out reconnaissance flights, affording a bird's-eye view of the battlefield and enemy positions. In September 1914, it was French pilots flying over enemy lines who watched two advancing German units change direction, opening a gap between them and setting the stage for the Battle of the Marne. From then on, both sides used aircraft to

British and German planes engage in a free-for-all dogfight (the German planes are marked with a black cross).

observe enemy troop movements, direct artillery fire, and photograph enemy lines.

Reconnaissance flights soon led to aerial combat. Pilots tried to knock each other out of the sky, maneuvering to gain command of the air over the battlefield. To begin with, pilots went aloft carrying passengers who fired at enemy planes with rifles and shotguns. Then light machine guns, mounted on the fronts of planes, were equipped with "interrupter" gears that allowed the guns to fire through the propellers without hitting the blades. To hit an opposing plane, the pilot had to fly directly at it.

These dogfights in the sky between daredevil pilots in open cockpits without seat belts, high above the mud of the trenches, were greatly admired. A pilot who shot down ten enemy planes qualified as an "ace" and was hailed as a national hero. The war's highest-scoring ace was a German, Baron Manfred von Richthofen. Called the Red Baron because his plane was painted red, he brought down eighty Allied aircraft before his luck ran out and he himself was shot down and killed. Eddie Rickenbacker, America's leading ace, flew during the final six months of the war and was credited with twenty-six aerial victories, an American record that stood until World War II.

Aircraft were also pressed into service as bombers. In 1915, Germany's lighter-than-air dirigible balloons, called Zeppelins after their designer, Count Ferdinand Zeppelin, began nighttime bombing raids over southern England, causing widespread panic and killing or wounding several thousand people. The Zeppelin crews simply dropped their bombs over the side of the passenger

Top: Captain Eddie Rickenbacker, America's leading air ace, standing up in his Spad fighter plane, October 1918. Rickenbacker, a former race car driver, served again in World War II.

Bottom: A German pilot drops a bomb over the side of his plane.

British antiaircraft gunners race to their guns on the outskirts of Armentières, France, March 1916.

gondola by hand. In later models, the bombs were released by an automatic mechanism.

The huge, slow-moving dirigibles were later replaced by more reliable long-range airplanes, such as the German Gotha bombers that carried out daylight raids on London. Then as now, air raids sometimes hit unintended targets. In July 1916, a French air raid on the German town of Karlsruhe mistakenly dropped its bombs on a circus, killing 154 children.

During the four years of the war, airplane technology was transformed. Today, designing and building a new airplane can take decades; back then, it took weeks. "We literally thought of and designed and flew the airplanes in a space of about six or eight weeks," said British aviation pioneer Thomas Sopwith. Aircraft became specialized as reconnaissance planes, fighters, bombers, and planes equipped to fly low and strafe enemy troops on the ground. History's first aerial bombing and sinking of a ship at sea took place in February 1916, when a German bomber sank a British freighter. The first antiaircraft guns were installed orig-

inally on ships, and then on land. And the first aircraft carrier made its debut on July 7, 1918, when seven British bombers took off from the deck of HMS *Furious* to attack two German Zeppelin sheds, destroying both the sheds and the dirigibles inside.

Airplanes and modern weaponry brought an end to the traditional role of cavalry. Since the days of Alexander the Great, mounted troops had proved decisive in offensive warfare and had served as an army's eyes, ranging far afield on reconnaissance missions. Every army that went to war in 1914 included huge numbers of men on horseback. The Russians, with twenty-four cavalry divisions, had over a million horses.

As the war progressed, cavalry proved no match for machine guns. And the stalemate on the Western Front, with entrenched armies dug in and facing each other across no man's land, made the cavalry almost useless. Aircraft took over the reconnaissance operations that cavalry could no longer perform.

When the fighting spilled over into the Middle East, cavalry for a time dominated the battlefield. The sweeping British victory at Megiddo (in present-day Israel) in September 1918, completing the British conquest of Turkish-occupied Palestine, was the last time in Western military history that mounted troops played a leading role. Horses, however, continued to pull guns and equipment, foot soldiers continued to walk, and armies still moved no faster than those of the distant past.

Communications technology in 1914 wasn't advanced enough to meet the needs of modern warfare. Radar and television did not yet exist. Wireless telegraphy, as radio was then called, required equipment that was too heavy and cumbersome to be carried into battle. Battlefield commanders depended on telephones to gather information and issue orders, yet telephone cables were easily broken during combat. Armies still relied on signal lamps and carrier pigeons to deliver messages that could mean the difference between life and death.

A British sentry keeps watch in a frontline trench while his comrades sleep, July 1916.

7

LIFE AND DEATH
IN THE TRENCHES

"We went through the broken trees to the east of the village and up a long trench to Battalion Headquarters," wrote author Robert Graves, recalling the night he joined his frontline unit in France as a twenty-one-year-old British officer. "The wet and slippery trench ran through dull red clay. I had a torch [a flashlight] with me, and saw that hundreds of field mice and frogs had fallen into the trench but found no way out. The light dazzled them, and because I could not help treading on them, I put the torch back in my pocket. We had no mental picture of what the trenches would be like."

Trench warfare was not what eager volunteers had expected when they signed up to fight on the Western Front. But as the year 1915 began, the opposing armies were deadlocked and trenches had become the dominating feature of the war.

German armies had occupied most of Belgium and penetrated deep into France.

The German strategy was to hold fast, to dig in and defend their entrenched positions, while at the same time attacking the battered Russian army in the east, inflicting enough losses on the Russians to knock them out of the war. Germany could then concentrate its forces in the west, where German generals were convinced the war would be decided. The Allies were just as convinced that Allied troops could achieve a breakthrough in the west, attacking enemy positions and driving the Germans back across their own border.

All along the Western Front, German armies worked at strengthening their positions, digging elaborate systems of trenches protected by barbed-wire entanglements and by batteries of machine guns and artillery. The challenge facing the French and British armies, hunkered down in their own deep entrenchments, was to launch attacks across no man's land—to break into and through the zigzagging mazes of enemy fortifications, which in places were miles deep.

The design of the trenches varied from place to place according to the terrain, but the basic pattern was similar everywhere: Facing no man's land were the heavily manned frontline trenches, deep enough to shelter a man standing upright, narrow enough to provide some protection from plunging enemy artillery shells. Several hundred yards to the rear were support trenches, holding men and supplies that could immediately move up to the front. Farther back still, beyond the range of all but the biggest enemy artillery, was a third system of trenches for the reserves.

The trenches did not run in straight lines but were broken by sharp twists and turns to prevent enemy troops who entered from commanding more than a limited range of rifle fire. Connecting these trenches were communication trenches, which allowed relief parties to reach the frontline under cover all the way from the rear. And excavated deep beneath the surface, where the soil allowed, were shell-proof underground shelters, or dugouts in places thirty or more feet deep, approached down wooden staircases.

Entire units could lose their way while navigating this interlocking maze of trenches and dugouts. Relief troops were escorted by guides who knew every twist and turn of the trench system. At crucial intersections, signboards were posted, pointing the way.

Mud and rain could make some trenches uninhabitable. "One night . . . there was a tremendous storm blowing, lightning was flashing and flares were still going up," British rifleman Henry Williamson recalled. "Rain splashed up about nine or ten inches in no man's land, and it went on and on and on. . . . The conditions of the latrines can be imagined and we could not sleep, every minute was like an hour. The dead were lying out in front. The

Rain and mud made many trenches and dugouts uninhabitable. This British sergeant was photographed in a flooded dugout in January 1917.

rains kept on, we were in yellow clay. . . . Our trenches were 7 ft. deep. We walked about or moved very slowly in . . . yellow watery clay. When the evening came and we could get out of it, it took about an hour to climb out. Some of our chaps slipped in and were drowned. They couldn't even be seen, but were trodden on later."

Trenches were constantly under repair. They were reinforced with sandbags, with sheets of corrugated iron, with wooden frames supporting the raised earthen parapets that protected the soldiers from enemy fire. Underfoot, some trench interiors were floored with wooden walkways called duckboards. And bit by bit, some underground living quarters, particularly those occupied by officers, were outfitted with such domestic comforts as electric lights, plank floors, fixed bedsteads, even carpets and pictures. When Robert Graves, led by a guide through a maze of underground passages, finally arrived at his company headquarters, his hands "were sticky with the clay from the side of the trench, and my legs soaked up to the calves," but he found "a two-room timber-built shelter in the side of a trench connecting the front and support lines," with a cloth-covered table, an ornamental lamp, "shelves with books and magazines, and bunks in the next room."

Officers and men alike shared their trenches with rats and frogs, with slugs and horned beetles that burrowed into the trench walls, with lice that infested every man's clothing. Rats as big as cats scampered across sleeping men's faces at night and chewed through their clothing to get at the food in their pockets. Soldiers tried to rid the trenches of rats by shooting them, bayoneting them, and clubbing them to death, but it was hopeless. A single pair of rats could produce more than eight hundred offspring in a year, spreading infection and contaminating food.

"There are five families of rats in the roof of my dug-out," British captain Bill Murray wrote to his family, "which is two feet

above my head in bed, and the little rats practice somersaults continuously through the night, for they have discovered that my face is a soft landing when they fall."

Blood-sucking lice, breeding in the seams of clothing, spread from one man to the next. Their bites left itchy red marks on the skin of just about every soldier. Ninety-five percent of British soldiers coming off the line were infested with lice.

Lice carried an infectious disease called trench fever, characterized by chills and high fever, which put thousands of men out of action. Trench foot, a painful fungal infection, was brought on by standing in cold, wet mud for days and nights while wearing field boots. When relief troops arrived at the front, "scores of men [suffering from trench foot] could not walk back from the trenches, but had to crawl, or to be carried [piggyback] by their

Six French soldiers face the camera in a dugout cut deep into the ground, reinforced with heavy timbers, and furnished with a table, benches, and an improvised stove, October 1915. Note the bottle of wine on the shelf.

A German soldier washes his feet in a trench in preparation for an inspection. Having wet feet for a long period could cause trench foot, a painful fungal infection.

comrades," reported Philip Gibbs, a British war correspondent. "So I saw hundreds of them, and as the winter dragged on, thousands." And many men also suffered from trench mouth, a severe bacterial infection of the gums, another hazard of life in the trenches, caused by poor diet, poor hygiene, and smoking.

Added to these indignities was the awful stench that hung over the frontlines, a foul odor that instantly assaulted visitors. You could smell the frontline miles before you could see it. The reek rose from rotting corpses lying in shallow graves, from overflowing latrines, and from the stale sweat of men who had not enjoyed the luxury of a bath for weeks.

Men grew accustomed to the smells, but they could never forget the artillery shells constantly raining down on them from enemy guns. It has been estimated that a third of the Allied casualties on the Western Front were suffered by men in trenches. Death could come suddenly, in a blinding flash, as shells exploded in or near the trenches, or from a well-aimed sniper's bullet as a soldier peered over a trench parapet into no man's land.

"In this sunshine," wrote Max Plowman in his memoir of the war, "it seems impossible to believe that at any minute we in this trench, and they in that, may be blown to bits by shells fired from guns at invisible distances by hearty fellows who would be quite ready to stand you a drink if you met them face to face."

Out beyond the frontline trenches, no man's land separating the opposing armies might be anywhere from a mile or more across to barely twenty-five yards wide. This menacing wasteland was pitted with shell craters, scarred by the charred remains of dead trees, often littered with debris and dead bodies. It wasn't always possible to carry the dead back to their trenches. By day, nothing seemed to move out there, but at night no man's land came alive with patrols that went out at dusk and returned at dawn. Men crawled out of their trenches to repair strands of barbed wire or to clear a path through the wire for a planned attack the next morning. Soldiers manned forward listening posts, eavesdropping near enemy lines, trying to pick up vital intelligence.

Raiding parties went out at night, hoping to bring back prisoners. Watching a raid while peering over the top of a British trench was "a hair-raising affair at the start, for our field guns had so little clearance that the [draft] of their shells could be felt on the back of one's neck. What was to be seen was like nothing else. Against the night there was a wild dance of red fan-shaped spurts of fire seen through a thickening haze." There was always the chance that men moving through the darkness of no man's land might be suddenly silhouetted by an enemy flare and targeted by machine guns.

Because no one could be expected to endure these perils for long, men were rotated on a regular schedule whenever possible. A battalion would spend perhaps a week on the frontline and would then be pulled back for a stint at the support line, then moved to the reserve line, and finally shunted to the rear before returning to the front for another cycle.

Under the stress of trench warfare, some soldiers seemed to suffer nervous breakdowns, a condition that became known as shell shock. Without having received physical injuries of any kind, men might begin to tremble or shake uncontrollably; some became like zombies, staring blankly into the distance as though in a trance. At first, battlefield commanders tended to dismiss shell shock as nothing more than rank cowardice. Some victims were court-martialed and even shot for desertion. But medical doctors increasingly viewed shell shock as a serious disorder, an understandable reaction to feelings of utter helplessness when on the receiving end of a bombardment, or when ordered to climb out of a hole in the face of blanketing machine-gun fire and risk sudden death.

By the end of the war, tens of thousands of shell-shock cases

Canadian soldiers write letters and sleep in their frontline trench, April 1918. Nighttime in the trenches was usually the busiest time, when reconnaissance patrols, wiring crews, and raiding parties went out under cover of darkness. During daylight hours, soldiers often had a chance to relax and catch a little sleep.

had been recorded. Victims often recovered sufficiently to be returned to action, and many performed heroically when they did. Others suffered nightmares and panic attacks for the rest of their lives, and some shell-shock victims were confined to insane asylums.

For all the hazards—the risks from sniper fire and incoming shells, the serious health problems—trenches saved lives. The best protection against enemy firepower was the dugout, the deeper the better. The greatest danger came when men crawled out of their trenches to "go over the top" and attack.

Opposite: A British chaplain conducts a field burial service in a frontline trench.

Canadian troops go "over the top" during a training exercise in France, October 1916.

8

OVER THE TOP

"Then, it was just five minutes to go—then zero—and all hell broke loose," recalled British sergeant-major Richard Tobin. "There was our barrage, then the German barrage, and over the top we went. As soon as we got over the top the fear and the terror left us. You don't look, you see; you don't listen, you hear; your nose is filled with fumes and death and you taste the top of your mouth. You are one with your weapon, the veneer of civilization has dropped away and you see just a line of men and a blur of shells."

The task facing the French and British armies was to break through German defenses, recover the lost territories of France, and liberate Belgium. Throughout 1915, the Allies launched a succession of attacks that cost thousands of lives and yielded little or no gain.

In this actual combat shot, French troops (at top) attack a German position in 1917. The French soldier at the center of the photo has been shot and is about to fall.

Masses of soldiers storming an enemy position protected by earthworks, barbed wire, and machine guns stood little chance of success unless they advanced behind a moving curtain of artillery fire—a barrage that could flatten wire entanglements and annihilate enemy troops in their trenches. And even when the attackers managed to reach the first line of opposing trenches, they seldom could penetrate beyond, for they themselves became vulnerable to enemy artillery and counterattacks. Hand-to-hand fighting with bayonets and hand grenades added to the slaughter. The battles seesawed back and forth, favoring first one side then the other, while neither side achieved a decisive victory and the casualties mounted.

The ghost village of Neuve-Chapelle in northern France after its capture by the British, March 1915.

At the Battle of Neuve-Chapelle in March 1915, "It was foggy and the attack was delayed two hours, which didn't do our spirits much good," British corporal Alan Bray recalled. "Then the time came for us to go over. We had to run forward about fifty yards, up some planks over our own front-line trenches, and then across a meadow where it was almost impossible to run; we could only stagger along. As we were going over these planks, about half of us were knocked out—either killed or wounded—and going across the meadow there were a lot more killed.

"When we finally stopped and lay down, trying to get what shelter we could from the tremendous rifle fire which was coming over, a sergeant just in front of me jumped up and said, 'Come on men, be British.' So we jumped up again and followed him. He ran about six yards and then he went down too.

"Well, then there were about a dozen of us left and we ran on another twenty yards towards the German trenches. Those trenches were literally packed—the men were standing four deep, firing machine-guns and rifles straight at us . . . [we] found ourselves looking straight up at the German trenches while they were firing straight down, gradually picking us off. Eventually there were only myself and another chap that weren't hit."

After three days and nights under fire at Neuve-Chapelle, British troops were so exhausted that they fell asleep. According to the official British history of the battle, they "could only be aroused by the use of force—a process made very lengthy by the fact that the battlefield was covered with British and German dead, who, in the dark, were indistinguishable from the sleepers."

When the battle was over, the British had succeeded in capturing just 1,200 yards of ground and what was now the ghost village of Neuve-Chapelle, while suffering more than 11,000 casualties. "I was wounded in the battle and taken to a casualty clearing station," trooper Walter Becklade of the Fifth Cavalry Brigade recorded. "I was beside a fellow who had got his arms bandaged up—I'd simply got my right arm bandaged. He was trying to light his pipe but couldn't get on very well so I offered to fill and light it for him. But when I'd lit it I suddenly realized he had nowhere to put it, as he'd had his lower jaw blown away. So I smoked the pipe and he smelt the tobacco, that was all the poor chap could have."

Even during lulls in the fighting, it was impossible to escape the sight and smell of death. Private Jack Mackenzie of the Cameron Highlanders wrote to his wife in Scotland: "We relieved our fourth battalion in here, these are the trench[es] which they lost so many men in capturing, & is just one vast deadhouse, the stench in some places is something awfull, the first thing we had to do was dig the trenches deeper & otherwise repair them & we came across bodies all over the place . . . but we have buried the most of them properly now. The ground behind us is covered yet by dead Camerons and Germans who fell on the seventeenth of May & we go out at night & bury them, it is a rotten job as they are very decomposed, but it has to be done . . . and we think it only right to their relatives at home, to put their poor bodies under the ground properly."

"I'd never seen a dead man and was very afraid of seeing anybody killed in front of my eyes," British lieutenant Robert Talbot Kelly remembered. To overcome his fears, he climbed down into an abandoned German trench that had been fought over weeks before and was now behind the British frontline:

"I wandered along this old German trench for a bit and was very interested in the way it was made. . . . Then suddenly round the bend in the trench I came to a great bay which was full of dead Germans, but they weren't a bit horrible. They had been dead for about six weeks and weather and rats and maggots and everything else had done their stuff. Now they were just shiny skeletons in their uniforms held together by the dry sinews, that wound round their bones. They were still wearing their uniforms

Death on the wire in no man's land: These French troops were shot as they attempted to cut a path through German barbed-wire defenses.

and still in the attitude in which they had died, possibly from a great shell burst. It was a most weird and extraordinary picture and I was absolutely fascinated. A skull, you know, grins at you in a silly way, it laughs at you and more or less says: 'Fancy coming here all terrified of dead men, look how silly we look.'"

In September 1915, the Allies launched a major offensive in France, hoping to break through enemy lines, drive the Germans back to the Meuse River, and end the war. French forces attacked in the Champagne region, while the British stormed German defenses in the mining area around the town of Loos. In both sectors, the attacks were preceded by the discharge of chlorine gas—the first time poison gas had been used by the Allies. At Loos, the gas hung over no man's land and drifted back into the

The Battle of Loos: British troops, photographed from the trench they have just left, advance through a cloud of poison gas, September 1915.

British trenches, sickening hundreds of men and holding up their advance.

Later at Loos, thousands of British troops advancing across an open field were slaughtered by German machine-gun fire. The Germans, appalled by the carnage, held their fire as the surviving British troops turned and retreated.

"Coming back over the ground that had been captured that day, the sight that met our eyes was quite unbelievable," British corporal Edward Glendinning recalled. "If you can imagine a flock of sheep lying down sleeping in a field, the bodies were as thick as that. Some of them were still alive, and they were crying out, begging for water and plucking at our legs as we went by. One hefty chap grabbed me around both knees and held me. 'Water, water,' he cried. I was just going to take the cork out of my water-bottle—I had a little left—but I was immediately hustled on by the man behind me. 'Get on, get on, we are going to get lost in no man's land, come on.' So it was a case where compassion had to give way to discipline and I had to break away from this man to run up to catch up with the men in front."

By the time the joint Allied offensive was called off in November, after several weeks of fighting, the French and British had suffered a quarter of a million casualties and had accomplished nothing.

Elsewhere in Europe, 1915 was a terrible year for the Allies. A disintegrating Russian army had been forced into a massive retreat across the entire Eastern Front. The Russians had abandoned Warsaw and been driven out of Poland and Galicia, giving up everything they had gained since the start of the war. General Nicholas Yanushkevich, the Russian chief of staff, complained that his armies were "melting like snow" before the German offensives. By the end of 1915, the Russians had lost about

Russian troops break and run during a battle in Galicia on the Eastern Front.

4 million men. Erich von Falkenhayn, the German army chief of staff, told Kaiser Wilhelm that the czar's army was "so weakened by the blows it has suffered that Russia need not be seriously considered a danger in the foreseeable future."

As the Russians retreated in Poland, abandoning town after town to the Germans, terrified refugees were fleeing in all directions. "All the villagers have been ordered to evacuate," wrote Ernst Nopper, a German officer. "They are in despair, and protest bitterly. At eight in the evening we are on the march again. We come out onto the road. It is dark. But what's that noise? Oh my God, what's happening on the road ahead? It is blocked by carts, full of kids and household stuff. The cows are bellowing, the dogs are barking and yelping. The poor people are going God knows where, anywhere to get away from the fighting. But the old nags don't have the strength to pull the loads; the air is filled with the sound of horses being whipped . . . and still the carts won't move. We don't have the heart just to drive through them. It's such a heartbreaking scene, we drag one cart after another out of the mud, get them onto the main road and then onto the bridge over the river Narew. I pity them all, particularly the little children, sitting in the carts or in their mothers' arms. They don't understand what is happening around them."

Italy, meanwhile, after renouncing its treaty agreements with the Central Powers, had entered the war on the side of the Allies. Drawn by the promise of territorial gains, the Italians had attacked the Austrians along the Isonzo, a mountain river running through a deep valley just inside Austria along its border with Italy, in what is now Slovenia. But the Italian army proved woefully unprepared for war, launching repeated attacks against the Austrians, gaining no ground, suffering huge casualties, and becoming a liability rather than an asset to the Allies.

The little Balkan nation of Bulgaria, watching the Italian and Russian setbacks, threw in its lot with the Central Powers. In October, a combined Austrian-German-Bulgarian invasion finally succeeded in crushing Serbia, occupying the kingdom and driving the defeated remnants of the Serbian army out completely.

But the biggest blow to the Allied cause in 1915 was the failure of the Gallipoli campaign, an attempt to force Turkey out of the war and to open a supply route from the Mediterranean to southern Russia. The Gallipoli Peninsula in Turkey commanded the entrance to the heavily fortified Dardanelles, the narrow waterway connecting the Aegean Sea with the Black Sea and Russia beyond. In an attempt to gain control of this strategic channel,

Above: An Australian soldier carries a wounded comrade to a first-aid station.

Overleaf: Australian troops charge a Turkish position on the Gallipoli Peninsula, 1915.

British, Australian, and New Zealand troops landed on the peninsula in April, while French troops staged a diversionary landing to the south. In August, the Allies made a second landing at Suvla Bay on the peninsula, suffering heavy losses. The Turks unexpectedly put up a fierce resistance, and for months the Allies were unable to break away from their narrow beachhead positions while the death rate mounted as a result of fighting and rampant disease. In December, the Allies began an orderly withdrawal, leaving Turkey still in control of the Dardanelles and still in the war. Total casualties on both sides were around a half million.

By the end of 1915, all hopes for a short war had vanished. With the Russians almost written off by both sides, it seemed increasingly likely that the war would be decided on the Western Front.

A German infantryman aims his rifle from a ruined trench near Fort Vaux during the Battle of Verdun, 1916. Beside him, a dead French soldier lies sprawled out, partly covered by debris.

9

THE BATTLE OF VERDUN

At 7:12 a.m. on February 21, 1916, an explosive shell fired from a German long-barreled gun nearly twenty miles away smashed into the thousand-year-old cathedral of Verdun. For the next nine hours—all morning and into the late afternoon—explosives rained down on the French troops guarding the little city and the ring of forts around it, a bombardment on a scale never before seen in any war. "No line is to remain unbombarded," the German orders commanded, "no possibilities of supply unmolested, nowhere should the enemy feel himself safe."

Verdun, nestled in a loop of the Meuse River in northern France, had little strategic importance in itself. But its symbolic value was immense. A fortress since Roman times, it was an honored historic site associated with French military glories and national pride. Until now, the war's battles had flowed around Verdun, bypassing the

At Verdun, German general Erich von Falkenhayn was determined to break the French army's will to fight.

city and its fortress. But Verdun lay close to the German border. It was exposed to attack from three sides. And it was the place chosen by German general Erich von Falkenhayn to deliver a shattering blow to the French army and break France's will to fight.

"The strain on France has reached [the] breaking point—though it is certainly borne with the most remarkable devotion," Falkenhayn wrote. "If we succeed in opening the eyes of her people to the fact that in a military sense they have nothing more to hope for, that breaking point would be reached."

Falkenhayn's plan was to strike at a vital location that the French could not afford to lose. They would defend Verdun at all costs, Falkenhayn reasoned, and would fight to regain the city if it was lost. By attacking Verdun, the Germans would "compel the French to throw in every man they have. If they do so the forces of France will bleed to death."

The attacking Germans would suffer losses too, but these would be kept to a minimum, Falkenhayn believed, by the element of surprise and by the hundreds of German guns massed in the hills north of Verdun.

Called "Operation Judgment" by the Germans, the Battle of Verdun would become the longest battle of World War I and one of the bloodiest ever fought. Beginning on February 21, daily German bombardments pulverized the battle zone as French troops cowered in trenches and dugouts, trying to make themselves as small as possible, praying not to be blown to bits or buried alive. Each day, as soon as the artillery barrage was lifted, German infantry troops, some equipped with flamethrowers, swept forward to attack. The French battled to hold their ground with rifle and machine-gun fire, then with grenades, and finally—in hand-to-hand fighting in the trenches—with gun butts and stones.

Caught by surprise, as Falkenhayn had planned, and overwhelmed by the enemy's numbers and firepower, the French began to fall back as the Germans advanced toward the key forts of Vaux and Douaumont. "The commanding officer and all company commanders have been killed," a French lieutenant signaled to army headquarters. "My battalion is reduced to approximately 180 men [from 600]. I have neither ammunition nor food. What am I to do?"

On February 24, German troops overran the entire outer trench zone. On the twenty-fifth, they captured Fort Douaumont on the heights overlooking Verdun. The city, which seemed on the point of falling, was being evacuated.

That evening, General Philippe Pétain arrived to assume command of the French forces. Pétain was not a man to give up. "Retake immediately any piece of land taken [by the Germans]," he insisted. The next day he issued his famous order, "They shall not pass!" a rallying cry that bolstered French morale.

Pétain reorganized the French defenses and took personal command of the artillery; now the Germans became the target of fierce bombardments as they clung to their frontline positions or tried to advance. Meanwhile, French reinforcements were pouring into the battle zone. And as Pétain had ordered, French troops fought to hang on to every yard of territory and counterattacked to regain ground that had been lost.

Falkenhayn had intended to wage a war of attrition: to bleed the French forces to death, maximizing French casualties while keeping German losses to a minimum. But he had not counted on the fervor of the French troops—on their determination to defend their home soil—and French soldiers inflicted as many losses on the Germans as the French themselves suffered. German troops advanced to within four miles of Verdun, but as French resistance stiffened, the Germans were halted and could not push their positions forward.

The battle settled into yet another stalemate as the bombardments intensified and each side attacked and counterattacked again and again. The ruined village of Vaux changed hands thirteen

French General Philippe Pétain rallied his troops with the cry "They shall not pass!"

A French sentry at the entrance to Fort Vaux, which was captured by the Germans in June 1916 and recaptured by the French in November.

times in March, but for the moment, Fort Vaux itself remained in French hands. In April, the Germans attempted to capture a strategic height named Le Mort Homme, Dead Man's Hill, but were pushed back before they could reach the summit. Then German guns bombarded the hill for several days running. A French officer, Augustin Cochin, spent six days in the Mort Homme trenches, "the last two days soaked in icy mud, under terrible bombardment, without any shelter other than the narrowness of the trench. . . . I arrived there with 175 men, I returned with 34, several half mad . . . not replying any more when I spoke to them."

As casualties mounted, Pétain did his best to spare his troops by rotating them in and out of the battle zone. Units at the front were sent to the rear for recuperation, while fresh units took their place. Eventually, three-fourths of the entire French army—125 divisions—would be rotated through Verdun.

The city's lifeline was a narrow road 72 kilometers (45 miles) long connecting Verdun with the town of Bar-le-Duc. Along this road an endless chain of trucks, cars, vans, ambulances, and other vehicles, following one after another every sixteen seconds, moved in and out of the fortress city, transporting 50,000 tons of equipment and 90,000 men per week. Today, helmet-topped road markers line the route, which has gone down in history as the Voie Sacrée, the Sacred Way.

The Germans continued to attack wherever they could. Early in June, they finally captured Fort Vaux after surrounding it and blowing it up section by section. The garrison surrendered only because the men had no water and were literally dying of thirst.

The Germans now pushed forward toward the surviving French fort of Souville, just two and a half miles from Verdun. On June 22, German troops opened their attack on the fort with a bombardment of explosives and a new kind of phosgene gas,

French supply trucks on the Voie Sacrée, the Sacred Way. When the road was running at full capacity, one vehicle passed a given point every sixteen seconds.

called Green Cross, which killed plants and insects as well as men and horses. The next day, 30,000 German infantrymen began their assault on the fort.

"It's hell, we are getting hit more and more often, as our position is the favorite enemy target . . . we expect an attack at any moment," wrote French lieutenant Henri Desagneaux, who had spent fourteen days in the trenches and somehow managed to write in his journal. "Our heads are buzzing, we have had enough. . . . Numb and dazed, without saying a word, and with our hearts pounding, we await the shell that will destroy us. The wounded are increasing in numbers around us. . . . There's death everywhere. At our feet, the wounded groan in a pool of blood; two of them, more seriously hit are breathing their last. One, a machine-gunner, has been blinded, with one eye hanging out of its socket and the other torn out; in addition he has lost a leg. The second has no face, an arm blown off, and a horrible wound in the stomach. Moaning and suffering atrociously, one begs me, 'Lieutenant, don't let me die, Lieutenant, I'm suffering, help me.' The other, perhaps more gravely wounded and nearer to death, implores me to kill him with these words, 'Lieutenant, if you don't want to, give me your revolver!' . . . For hours, these groans and supplications continue until, at 6 p.m., they die before our eyes without anyone being able to help them."

For nearly three weeks, French troops beat back successive enemy attacks on Fort Souville. The Germans made one final ef-

Two views of Verdun after months of German bombardment.

A wounded soldier is unloaded from a French ambulance at Verdun.

fort to capture the fort on July 11, reaching its walls before they were driven off. This was the last German attack.

By then, 20 million shells had been fired into the battle zone, creating a ghostly landscape of pockmarked fields and charred and splintered forests. Entire villages had disappeared; some would never be rebuilt. Verdun itself was a smoldering ruin, but it remained in French hands. A half million men, French and German, had been wounded or killed fighting over an ancient fortress that had small strategic value.

The Germans had failed in their intention to make the French army "bleed to death." Even if they had captured Verdun, they would have gained little. For the French, saving Verdun had been a matter of national pride.

For the time being, the fighting at Verdun was over. Meanwhile, another nightmarish battle, raging since the beginning of July, had shifted the center of action on the Western Front from Verdun to the Somme River.

British troops with wire cutters attached to their rifles pause on their way to the front on July 1, 1916, the first day of the Battle of the Somme. More than half of the men who entered no man's land that day were listed as killed, missing, or wounded.

10

THE BATTLE
OF THE SOMME

The Allies had agreed on a plan to break the stalemate. French, British, Russian, and Italian armies were to launch a joint offensive in several areas, east and west, attacking the Central Powers from all sides and preventing them from shifting their reserves from one front to another.

The offensive on the Western Front was to be carried out by French and British forces along the Somme River, north of Verdun in the province of Picardy. Originally, the plan called for equal participation by the French and British, but with so many French troops engaged at Verdun, the British took over the major role on the Somme. France would contribute three divisions to the campaign, while Britain had nineteen divisions.

The British commander, Sir Douglas Haig, had planned every move down to the last detail. A massive infantry attack would be preceded by a weeklong artillery bombardment in which a million and a half shells would be fired, flattening the enemy's barbed-wire defenses, destroying their trenches and fortifications, and stunning any enemy soldiers who managed to survive. The attacking Allied troops could then advance across no man's land behind the shield of a creeping barrage. They would take possession of the enemy trenches, which should be empty by the time they arrived, and move beyond them to open country in the rear.

General Haig was supremely confident. "I feel that every step in my plan has been taken with the Divine help," he wrote to his wife on the eve of the battle. And he recorded in his diary, "The [barbed] wire has never been so well cut, nor artillery preparation so thorough."

But events did not play out as Haig had planned.

When British troops went over the top on the morning of July 1, 1916, most of them were not equipped for an infantry assault. Each man was weighed down with sixty pounds of equipment, including picks, shovels, and sandbags judged necessary to fortify enemy positions that, according to Haig's plan, had already been conquered for them by the artillery. This bulky load made it difficult enough to climb out of a trench, and harder still to move faster than a slow walk or to lie down to take shelter and then rise quickly.

"At 7:30 we went up the ladders, doubled through the gaps in the [British] wire, and lay down, waiting for the line to form up on each side of us," R. H. Tawney of the Seventh Division recalled. "When it was ready, we went forward, not doubling [marching twice as fast], but at a walk. For we had 900 yards of rough ground to the trench which was our first objective."

As the troops fanned out across no man's land, expecting little opposition, German machine gunners emerged unharmed from their underground dugouts and opened fire.

British general Douglas Haig persisted in attacking again and again.

"I see men arising and walking forward; and I go forward with them," rifleman Henry Williamson recalled, "in a glassy delirium wherein some seem to pause, with bowed heads, and sink carefully to their knees, and roll slowly over, and lie still. Others roll and roll, and scream and grip my legs in uttermost fear, and I have to struggle to break away, while the dust and earth on my tunic changes from grey to red.

"And I go on with aching feet, up and down across ground like a huge ruined honeycomb, and my wave melts away, and the second wave comes up, and also melts away, and then the third wave merges into the ruins of the first and second, and after a while the fourth blunders into the remnants of the others, and we begin to run forward to catch up with the [artillery] barrage, gasping and sweating, in bunches, anyhow, every bit of the months of drill and rehearsal forgotten, for who could have imagined that the 'Big Push' was going to be like this?"

Supporting troops scramble out of their trenches and move forward to attack German defenses.

A German soldier, Matthäus Gerster, described the attack as he saw it: "When the leading British line was within one hundred yards, the rattle of machine guns and rifle fire broke out from along the whole line of [German] craters. Some fired kneeling so as to get a better target over the broken ground, while others in the excitement of the moment, stood up regardless of their own safety to fire into the crowd of men in front of them. . . . The advance rapidly crumbled under this hail of shells and bullets. All along the line men could be seen throwing their arms into the air and collapsing, never to move again. Badly wounded rolled about in their agony, and others less severely injured crawled to the nearest shell-hole for shelter. . . .

"With all this were mingled the moans and groans of the wounded, the cries for help and the last screams of death."

The weeklong Allied bombardment had turned out to be far less effective than General Haig had predicted. Large numbers of the shells fired were duds; they failed to detonate. Those that did explode did not manage to destroy German defenses dug deep into the hillsides, sheltering waiting German troops. And the bombardment also failed to flatten the Germans' barbed-wire entanglements, merely tossing the barbed wire around and creating even more of a barrier than before. Finally, the crucial coordination between infantry and artillery broke down during the con-

Advancing to the attack through German barbed wire.

fusion of battle; the creeping barrage of exploding shells meant to precede and protect the advancing troops moved too fast and too far, leaving the troops exposed while they were still in no man's land on the wrong side of German barbed wire.

German soldiers fighting for their lives fired point-blank at the long lines of overloaded British troops plodding toward them. As the British approached German positions, they had to seek out gaps in the barbed wire and jam together as they crowded through, offering an easy target to German machine gunners. "When we started to fire we just had to load and reload," one of the machine gunners said. "They went down in their hundreds. We didn't have to aim, we just fired into them."

Some 100,000 British troops entered no man's land that day. Of those, more than 20,000 never returned; one man out of five was either dead or missing. Another 40,000 were wounded. It was the bloodiest day in the history of British warfare, the highest death toll in a single day of fighting during the entire war. Two German-held villages and one German stronghold were captured, but otherwise the twenty-five-mile front had scarcely changed. When darkness fell, the battle was already deadlocked.

Rescuing a comrade under fire. This image is a still from the British documentary film *The Battle of the Somme*. The rescued soldier died thirty minutes later.

Stretcher-bearers at the Battle of the Somme, September 1916.

German casualties that day, around 6,000, were a tenth of the British losses. At many places along the front, German troops were so appalled by the slaughter that when they realized their own lives were no longer at risk, they stopped firing so that British wounded could struggle back to their own lines. One German soldier called the day's battle "an amazing spectacle of unexampled gallantry, courage and bull-dog determination on both sides."

The Battle of the Somme continued for the next four months as the opposing armies fought bloody engagements over tiny patches of ground. General Haig's expectation of a breakthrough was never realized. Like Verdun, the Somme quickly became a war of attrition in which each side tried to wear down the other.

"One summer evening soon after the battle of the Somme had started," Captain Herbert Sulzbach, a German artillery officer, recalled, "the guns were rumbling and there was a terrible noise of battle in our ears. Yet where we lay, just thirty meters from the trenches, there were mountains and peace, and hardly any shooting. We could see the French soldiers, and one night a Frenchman started to sing—he was a wonderful tenor. None of us dared to shoot and suddenly we were all looking out from the trenches and applauding, and the Frenchman said 'Merci.' It was peace in the middle of war, and the strange thing was, that just a few kilometers northwards the terrible battle of the Somme was going on."

In September, the British introduced their new weapon, the tank, without much success. A fleet of thirty-six Mark I tanks lumbered into action, terrifying the Germans and leading a British advance of 3,500 yards before the tanks were knocked out by artillery fire or stopped by mechanical breakdowns in rough ground.

Allied forces continued their attacks, with little gain, until snowstorms and rain turned the Somme battlefield into a muddy morass. On November 19, the Allied offensive was officially called off. By then, the greatest Allied advance along the entire twenty-five-mile front had been seven miles, and the French and British had failed to break through the German lines. The Allies had lost more than 600,000 men, killed and wounded. German casualties were about 450,000.

Most of the British troops were inexperienced volunteers, men who had enlisted while Britain was raising a new army to fight in France, and who marched to the front singing rousing battle songs. They have been called an army of innocents. The Somme was their first experience of war; they offered up their lives in an epic battle that has haunted British memory ever since.

While the British and French were fighting the Germans at Verdun and the Somme, Russian and Italian troops battled the armies of Austria-Hungary on distant fronts. The Italians had been locked in futile combat along the Isonzo River in Austria since the summer of 1915, fighting a succession of inconclusive battles. In November 1916, the Ninth Battle of the Isonzo, like the previous eight, lasted only a few days and resulted in a heavy toll of killed and wounded for almost no gain of ground.

In the Balkans, Romania, a latecomer, entered the war on the side of the Allies and was quickly overrun by the Germans, who gained control of that country's valuable oil and grain resources.

The Russians, almost written off by both sides, surprised everyone. They launched an attack in Galicia under General Alexei Brusilov that overwhelmed Austro-Hungarian forces, captured huge numbers of prisoners, and recovered some of the territory lost during the Russian retreat the previous year. Brusilov's victory was the one successful contribution to the joint Allied offensive in 1916. It almost knocked Austria-Hungary out of the war. But it was won at the cost of a million Russian casualties, a staggering loss from which the czar's armies would never recover.

In the Middle East, British and Turkish forces clashed repeatedly in Mesopotamia (modern Iraq), which the British had invaded in 1914 in an effort to gain control of the oil refineries at Basra, at the head of the Persian Gulf. The Turks were also fighting the Russians in the wild mountains of the Caucasus, where an ill-equipped Turkish army suffered severely as the opposing sides struck at each other again and again.

Turkey's Armenian population, a vulnerable minority in the Ottoman Empire, suffered grievously during the war. For a century, the ancient kingdom of Armenia had been divided between Turkey and Russia. With those nations at war, Armenians living under Turkish rule, accused of aiding the Russians, were increasingly subject to persecution by the Turks. Beginning in 1915, hundreds of thousands of Armenians, forcibly removed from the border areas where they lived, either starved or were killed in what historians have called the first true genocide of the twentieth century.

At Verdun, meanwhile, after a summer standoff, the fighting flared up again. In October, the French moved to recover lost ground and recaptured Fort Douaumont. In December, they mounted another offensive and regained much of the ground lost earlier in the year. By the end of 1916, French and German troops were facing each other across a front that had scarcely changed since the fighting began in February.

On the Western Front alone, more than a half million men lost their lives in 1916. Second Lieutenant Alfred Joubaire, serving with the French 124th Regiment at Verdun, made the following entry in his diary on May 23, 1916: "Humanity is mad! It must be mad to do what it is doing. What a massacre. What scenes of horror and carnage! I cannot find words to translate my impressions. Hell cannot be so terrible. Men are mad!"

That was the last entry in Alfred Joubaire's diary. That day, or possibly the next, his life was ended by a German shell. He was twenty-one.

A German U-boat surfaces in the North Atlantic.

✦ 11 ✦

THE WAR AT SEA

With the land war deadlocked, Britain and Germany were each determined to achieve ultimate victory by winning the war at sea.

All the warring nations needed access to the outside world. Neither Britain nor Germany produced enough food to support its population. Both countries had to import raw materials to supply their war industries, and this was all done by ship. The British believed that by blockading German shipping lanes and seaports, they could starve Germany into submission.

The Germans had a similar plan. They were convinced that they could force Britain to abandon the war by disrupting Allied shipping before vessels could reach the British Isles.

Great Britain's Royal Navy had long dominated the world's oceans. Early in the war, British warships swept German shipping from the seas and clamped a total blockade on German seaports, cutting off most of Germany's imports. Germany retaliated by sending its fleet of submarines into action. Called U-boats (*Unterseebooten,* or undersea boats), submarines were the only German vessels that could venture safely into open waters. Within weeks of the war's outbreak, German U-boats had sunk three British cruisers in the English Channel, sending 1,500 sailors to their deaths.

The British declared the entire North Sea a war zone, in which even neutral ships would be stopped and searched; all goods destined for German ports would be seized and confiscated. The Germans in turn declared all approaches to the British Isles war zones; they would seek to destroy not only enemy warships but also hostile merchant ships, those carrying war supplies to Britain. And they would torpedo those ships without first providing for the safety of passengers and crew, in violation of international

Struck by a torpedo fired from the submarine in the foreground, a merchant steamer explodes and starts to sink. More than 7,000 Allied and neutral ships were sunk, damaged, or captured by German U-boats during the war.

A welcoming crowd greets the British passenger liner *Lusitania* as it arrives in New York for the first time, September 13, 1907.

agreements concerning naval warfare. Germany warned citizens of neutral countries not to board ships going into war zones. But Woodrow Wilson, the American president, insisted on full neutral trading rights with all the warring nations, and he refused to limit Americans' freedom to travel.

On May 1, 1915, the British luxury liner *Lusitania*, famed as the biggest and fastest ship in Atlantic service, sailed from New York on a voyage to England. That morning, New York newspapers carried an advertisement, placed by the German embassy in Washington, warning, "Travelers intending to embark on the Atlantic voyage . . . do so at their own risk." Germany had reason to believe that the *Lusitania* was carrying American-manufactured munitions as part of its cargo.

The *New York Times* announces the *Lusitania* disaster on the front page of its May 8, 1915, edition. The inset at bottom right shows the warning advertisement placed in the paper by the German embassy before the ship sailed. At bottom left, a sailor bows his head at the burial of some of the *Lusitania's* victims.

Six days later, on May 7, as the giant British steamship neared the end of a festive voyage, it turned into the path of a patrolling German submarine off the southern coast of Ireland and was torpedoed. The *Lusitania* sank in fifteen minutes.

"There was a dull, thudlike, not very loud but unmistakable explosion," Lady Margaret Mackworth recalled. "It seemed to come from a little below us and about the middle of the vessel on the port side. . . . As I ran up the stairs, the boat was already heeling over. As I ran, I thought, 'I wonder I'm not more frightened,' and then, 'I'm beginning to get frightened, but I musn't let myself.' . . .

"I saw that the water had come over on to the deck. We were

not, as I had thought, sixty feet above the sea; we were already under the sea. I saw the water green just about up to my knees. I do not remember its coming up further; that must all have happened in a second. The ship sank and I was sucked right down with her.

"The next thing I can remember was being deep down under the water. It was very dark, nearly black. I fought to come up. I was terrified of being caught on some part of the ship and kept down. . . . When I came to the surface I found that I formed part of a large, round, floating island composed of people and debris of all sorts, lying so close together that at first there was not very much water noticeable in between. People, boats, hencoops, chairs, rafts, boards, and goodness knows what besides, all floating cheek by jowl. . . . Many people were praying aloud in a curious, unemotional monotone; others were shouting for help in much the same slow impersonal chant: 'Bo-at . . . bo-at . . . bo-at. . . .'"

Lady Mackworth and her father were rescued. Of the 2,000 passengers on board, some 1,200 drowned, including many women and children. Among the victims were 128 Americans.

The sinking of the *Lusitania* shocked the American people, helped turn public opinion against Germany, and almost caused the United States to break off relations with Germany. But President Wilson was determined to preserve America's neutrality, and the sinking was diplomatically smoothed over. German newspapers defended the sinking as a justified act of war. "The English wish to abandon the German people to death by starvation," one German newspaper commented. "We are more humane. We simply sank an English ship with passengers who, at their own risk and responsibility, entered the zone of [war] operations."

Following the outcry over the *Lusitania,* Germany imposed strict limitations on submarine operations, pledging to warn those on board a vessel about to be attacked so they could abandon ship beforehand. German U-boats continued to torpedo Allied merchant ships, sinking between fifty and a hundred a month in 1915. But most ships managed to evade the prowling U-boats and made it safely to British shores. Britain was able to import sufficient food supplies until mid-1917, when the U-boat campaign intensified.

Germany and its ally Austria-Hungary did not fare as well under the British blockade. By 1916, food and clothing were becoming scarce in both countries. Food riots broke out in more than thirty German cities. Soap, fuel, and other necessities were strictly rationed. The winter of 1916–17 became known as the "turnip winter," when that humble vegetable became the staple of many diets. Hunger-related diseases such as rickets, scurvy, and tuberculosis were widespread, and in the cities, death from starvation was becoming a daily occurrence.

As the blockade of Germany caused increasing misery, a new German naval commander, Admiral Reinhard Scheer, lost patience. Germany's High Seas Fleet had been bottled up in port for nearly two years, unwilling to venture out and engage the British Grand Fleet, which was poised and waiting in the north

The Battle of Jutland: HMS *Invincible,* a British battle cruiser, explodes after being hit five times by shells from German warships, May 31, 1916.

of Scotland. On May 31, 1916, Admiral Scheer led the High Seas Fleet out into the North Sea to challenge the British Grand Fleet. The British steamed south to meet the challenge, and the two fleets clashed off the coast of Denmark in what became known as the Battle of Jutland—the biggest naval battle ever fought before World War II. More than 150 warships—dreadnaughts, battle cruisers, armored cruisers, light cruisers, destroyers—pressed forward into action, cannon blazing under the gray sky of the North Sea.

By the next morning, June 1, the Germans had lost eleven ships and 2,500 men. British losses were heavier: fourteen ships sent to the bottom with a loss of 6,200 men. Strategically, the battle changed nothing; it had almost no effect on the course of the war. The Germans withdrew to their home ports, where they remained, largely inactive, until the war ended. From then on, Germany's efforts to win a decisive victory at sea were conducted entirely with submarines.

Meanwhile, the British "hunger-blockade," as the Germans called it, was causing mounting demands for peace. Along with severe shortages of food and almost everything else, the shocking losses at Verdun and the Somme—a million and a half German soldiers dead and wounded—had shaken Germany's morale.

Members of the German naval staff were calling for a return to unrestricted submarine warfare—allowing U-boat captains to sink Allied shipping in international waters without warning. They were convinced that Germany's submarine fleet could destroy Britain's ability to wage war within a few months. "There can be no justification or military grounds for refusing any further to employ what promises to be our most effective weapon," Admiral Alfred von Tirpitz declared. "We should ruthlessly employ every weapon that is suitable for striking against England on her home ground."

An escaping crew member (top of photo) slides down a rope as a ship torpedoed by a German U-boat sinks beneath the waves and a lifeboat pulls away. Unrestricted submarine warfare helped draw the United States into the war.

Some German military leaders feared that unrestricted submarine warfare would bring the United States into the war, thus guaranteeing Germany's defeat. After a lengthy debate, the Germans decided to take the risk. "Fear of a break [with the U.S.]," argued Admiral Henning von Holtzendorff, "must not hinder us from using the weapon that promises success."

At the beginning of 1917, the German navy had about a hundred submarines available for action in the North Sea, the Atlantic, and the Mediterranean. U-boat captains were ordered to

begin unrestricted attacks against all vessels approaching the British Isles. The Germans hoped to win the war before the United States could intervene.

Woodrow Wilson had been reelected to a second term as president in 1916 with the campaign slogan "He kept us out of war." Most Americans did not want to become involved in a distant European war that seemed at first none of their business. But as the war progressed, American sympathies increasingly favored the Allies. Americans shared with Britain a language and many traditions, and with France historic ties going back to Lafayette and the Revolutionary War. Germany was seen as a militaristic threat because of its admittedly brutal actions in Belgium, its introduction of poison gas, and its use of unrestricted U-boat warfare—all magnified by Allied propaganda.

The United States, meanwhile, had become a major supplier of arms to the Allies—by this time, because of the blockade of German ports, the only available buyers. To finance their arms purchases, the Allies had borrowed more than two billion dollars from American banks, a debt that would never be repaid if Germany won the war.

Wilson's main concern had been to preserve America's neutrality. All along, he had been urging the warring nations to make peace. After his reelection, he attempted to arrange a peace conference, but the opposing sides could not agree on a basis for discussion, and the conference never took place. Both sides still felt that they could win the war and dictate their own peace terms.

A rush of events soon changed Wilson's attitude toward the war. On January 31, 1917, the German ambassador in Washington informed the American government that Germany was about to resume unrestricted submarine warfare against all vessels approaching the British Isles. The United States immediately broke off diplomatic relations with Germany. On February 26, after two Americans were drowned in the sinking of the British

President Woodrow Wilson addresses Congress. On April 2, 1917, after additional U-boat attacks on American ships, Wilson asked a special session of Congress to declare war on Germany. The Senate voted 82 to 6 in favor of war; in the House of Representatives, the vote was 373 to 50. War was formally declared on April 6.

liner *Laconia* by a German submarine, Wilson asked Congress for permission to begin arming American merchant ships.

Three days later, the publication of a bizarre message sent by the German foreign minister, Arthur Zimmermann, to the government of Mexico helped push the United States closer to war. Called the "Zimmermann telegram," the message proposed a military alliance between Germany and Mexico if the United States was to enter the war, with the promise that Mexico would be offered the chance to recover the lost territories of Texas, New Mexico, and Arizona. Intercepted and decoded by both British intelligence and the U.S. State Department, the message seemed so outrageous when it was published by American newspapers on March 1, 1917, that it was thought to be a forgery until Zimmermann himself acknowledged having sent it.

Publication of the Zimmermann telegram was followed by German U-boat attacks on four American ships, which were torpedoed without warning. That proved to be the tipping point. Speaking before a special session of Congress, President Wilson

declared that the German submarine campaign was a "war against all nations," and on April 6, 1917, the United States formally declared war on Germany. Declarations of war against Austria-Hungary, Bulgaria, and Turkey followed.

Wilson stated that the United States had entered the war because "the world must be made safe for democracy"—an admirable goal, but very different from the motives that had plunged Europe into war three years earlier.

The Battle of Arras: Forward observation officers of the British artillery, equipped with binoculars and a periscope, direct fire during the bombardment of German positions, April 8, 1917. One man uses a field telephone to relay messages back to the firing gun batteries.

12

MUTINY, REVOLUTION, AND THE COLLAPSE OF ARMIES

The United States had declared war but did not have an army capable of fighting alongside the French and British. The U.S. regular Army was small, with only 130,000 men, no tanks, and few aircraft. As a gesture, a token force of one infantry division and two Marine brigades would be sent to France right away. But it would take at least a year of recruitment, training, and transportation across the Atlantic before the Americans were ready to take the field in Europe.

On the Western Front, the stalemate continued. The Germans had pulled back to a heavily fortified position known to the British as the Hindenburg Line and to the Germans as the Siegfried Line. Allied generals still dreamed of achieving a dramatic breakthrough, but every attempt to breach the German defenses was frustrated and repulsed.

In April 1917, an offensive by British and Canadian troops at the city of Arras in northern France bogged down in sleet, snow, and ankle-deep mud. After several days of fighting, three British generals, alarmed by the heavy loss of life, defied army tradition by protesting directly to their superior, General Douglas Haig. But there was no question in Haig's mind that more gains could be made, and he ordered the attacks to continue.

The Battle of Arras dragged on until the middle of May before it was called off. A dent of four miles had been made in the German lines. But the only significant gain of ground had been the capture by the Canadians of the dominating Vimy Ridge near Arras. These limited results had cost 150,000 British casualties. The Germans suffered equally, but they quickly rebuilt their defensive positions, and the Arras sector returned to the stalemate still gripping the Western Front. Today, more than a hundred military cemeteries around Arras hold the remains of Allied soldiers killed in action there.

While the British were fighting at Arras, the French launched their own offensive 130 miles to the south across the Aisne River, aimed at a strategic wooded ridge called the Chemin des Dames (Ladies' Road). French general Robert Nivelle had predicted a "rupture," as he called it, in the German lines—a decisive blow that would end the war. Instead, his troops advanced with painful difficulty in snow, sleet, and mist, penetrating enemy lines by just a few miles and never reaching the deep German defenses. After ten blood-soaked days and 130,000 French casualties, including 29,000 killed, the offensive was abandoned and General Nivelle was removed from his command.

The failure of the Nivelle offensive was so demoralizing, it almost destroyed the fighting spirit of the French army. Following the defeat at the Chemin des Dames, French soldiers engaged in what historians have called "the mutinies of 1917." They weren't mutinies in the sense that soldiers attacked their officers, but were more like workmen's strikes, in which entire units refused to return to the trenches or take part in new attacks. The war so far had been fought at the cost of nearly a million French lives out of a male population of 20 million, a shocking death toll that had shaken the French resolve to fight in what increasingly seemed an endless conflict.

General Philippe Pétain, who replaced Nivelle as commander in chief, dealt with the mutiny more through persuasion than punishment. Several thousand soldiers were court-martialed and forty-nine were shot, but for the great majority of the men under his command, Pétain introduced reforms—longer periods of rest, more home leave, and better food. And he refrained for the moment from ordering further offensives. "I set about suppressing serious cases of indiscipline with the utmost urgency," Pétain explained. "I will maintain this repression firmly, but without forgetting that it applies to soldiers who have been in the trenches with us for three years and who are our soldiers."

For the remainder of 1917, French troops would hold the line against enemy attacks. They would defend their homeland, but they would not go over the top and attack.

While French soldiers engaged in "acts of collective indiscipline," as their commanders preferred to say, the Russian army was collapsing and Russia itself was in turmoil. At one time, most Russians were united in supporting the war effort. However, the corruption and incompetence of the czar's government, along with huge losses on the battlefronts, had eroded the army's morale and darkened the mood of the Russian public.

Early in 1917, acute shortages of food and fuel led to strikes and riots in Petrograd (formerly St. Petersburg), the Russian capital. When troops joined the demonstrators instead of firing on them, the riots turned to revolution. The army refused to support Czar Nicholas, and in March he was forced to give up his

A French soldier rests in a dugout behind the lines.

As strikes and riots swept Russia in March 1917, soldiers sided with the demonstrators, refused to support the czar, and voted to join the Russian Revolution.

throne—climaxing years of government repression, unrest, and revolutionary agitation.

A new liberal government under Alexander Kerensky vowed to continue the war for the defense of the Russian homeland. That summer, a brief Russian offensive faltered in the face of a German counterattack. Russian defenses crumbled, and the retreat became a headlong rout as entire units refused to fight. Soldiers deserted by the tens of thousands, voting for peace with their feet as they headed for home. In September 1917, as a German army moved toward the Russian capital, power began to slip from Kerensky's hands into those of a revolutionary leader named Vladimir Ilyich Lenin, head of the Bolshevik faction of the Russian Communist Party.

When the Communists finally seized control of the government in November, Lenin's calls for peace, bread, and land had overwhelming popular support. He immediately asked Germany for an armistice, thereby ending Russia's part in World War I. The new revolutionary government had proclaimed the "socialization" of land; as soldiers left the front to return to their villages and claim what they believed would be land for the taking, the Russian army did in fact begin to melt away.

In March 1918, after much delay and hesitation, the Russians signed the Treaty of Brest-Litovsk, surrendering to the Germans an area three times the size of Germany itself. This territory contained a quarter of Russia's population, a third of its agricultural land, and about half of its heavy industry. By then, the Germans had transferred the best units of their eastern army to the Western Front, where they were preparing for a new offensive against the French and British before the Americans arrived.

Another setback for the Allies was taking place along the Isonzo River in Austria's mountain borderland, where Italian and Austrian armies had been battling since the summer of 1915. With Russia's defeat, Germany was able to send reinforcements to the Austrians. In October 1917, near the little frontier town of Caporetto, the Austrians with their German allies achieved an unexpected breakthrough in what is called the Twelfth Battle of the Isonzo. The entire Italian front collapsed, depriving the Italians of gains they had won at great cost during the past two years. Retreating Italian troops were driven down from the mountains onto the plains as hundreds of thousands of soldiers surrendered or deserted, disappearing into the countryside. The Italians finally managed to regroup eighty miles to the rear along the Piave River, but the Italian army, like the French, would not return to the offensive until the following year.

———

With Russia in turmoil and the French army on strike, the Italian army suffered a devastating defeat in the rugged mountain region along Italy's border with Austria. In this photo, Italian heavy guns are being transported up a mountain road during the Twelfth Battle of the Isonzo.

On the Western Front during the summer and fall of 1917, the British fought what one historian has called "the most notorious campaign of the war," the Third Battle of Ypres, also known as the Battle of Passchendaele, after the Belgian village that was the ultimate objective of the British offensive and was totally destroyed during the fighting.

With the French army marking time, British general Haig was convinced that the outcome of the war depended on the armies under his command. Haig worried that the Americans would not arrive in time to prevent an Allied defeat. The British could win a decisive victory, he believed, by opening a new offensive in Belgian Flanders over the old battlefields around the ruined town of Ypres. The objective was to break through the German lines, advance to the Belgian coast, and capture the seaports used by German U-boats as their forward bases. Haig's offensive, fought by

British, Canadian, and ANZAC troops, opened with stunning success; it ended by almost breaking the heart of the British army.

The first objective was to capture Messines Ridge south of Ypres and use it as a jumping-off point for the main push toward the Belgian coast. For months, special British units had been secretly digging tunnels under the German positions, leading to nineteen underground chambers packed with a million pounds of explosives. Just before dawn on June 7, following a massive artillery bombardment, the explosives were detonated with a noise heard 140 miles away in London, turning the crest of Messines Ridge into a flaming volcano. When the attacking force reached the crest, the dazed defenders—those few who had survived—were unable to offer any resistance.

The assault on Messines Ridge was a spectacular tactical suc-

A British artillery observer watches as shells rain down on Messines Ridge in the distance, June 1917.

cess. But when the main British offensive opened at the end of July, the fighting quickly became another nightmarish battle, more horrifying and pointless than Verdun or the Somme. Heavy rains combined with continual bombardments from both sides turned the battlefield into an impassable morass of mud. "The ground is churned up to a depth of ten feet and is the consistency of porridge," reported a British artillery commander. "The middle of the shell craters are so soft that one might sink out of sight. . . . There must be hundreds of German dead buried here and now their own shells are reploughing the area and turning them up."

Wounded men died when they were unable to lift themselves out of the soft, shifting slime. Despite mounting casualties, Gen-

The village of Wytschaete near Ypres after its capture by the British on June 7, 1917.

eral Haig was determined to persist, no matter how wet the battlefield became. "The enemy is faltering," he told his commanders, "and . . . a good decisive blow might lead to decisive results."

A British officer, Edwin Vaughn, described the efforts of his
unit to move forward: "Up the road we staggered, shells bursting
all around us. A man stopped dead in front of me, and exasper-
ated I cursed him and butted him with my knee. Very gently he
said, 'I'm blind, Sir,' and turned to show me his eyes and nose
torn away by a piece of shell. 'Oh, God! I'm sorry, sonny,' I said.
'Keep going on the hard part,' and left him staggering back in the
darkness. . . .

"From other shell holes from the darkness on all sides came
the groans and wails of wounded men; faint, long, sobbing moans
of agony, and despairing shrieks. It was too horribly obvious that
dozens of men with serious wounds must have crawled for safety

Stretcher-bearers struggle through
mud up to their knees as they carry a
wounded soldier to safety, August 1917.

into new shell holes, and now the water was rising about them and, powerless to move, they were slowly drowning. Horrible visions came to me with those cries, [of men] lying maimed out there trusting that their pals would find them, and now dying terribly, alone amongst the dead in the inky darkness. And we could do nothing to help them."

After two days and nights on the battlefront, Vaughn's unit was relieved and he led his survivors back to the rear. The next morning, when he awoke and reported for muster, "my worst fears were realized. Standing near the [breakfast] cookers were four small groups of bedraggled, unshaven men from whom the quartermaster sergeants were gathering information concerning any of their pals they had seen killed or wounded. It was a terrible list . . . out of our happy little band of 90 men, only 15 remained."

An old French couple visit their former home and find a pile of stone and debris.

General Haig ordered his brave troops to battle on until the rubble of bricks that had once been the village of Passchendaele was finally captured by the Canadians on November 10, 1917. By then, the British had suffered 240,000 casualties, including 70,000 killed, for a gain of some five miles of Flanders mud.

The following March, Passchendaele would be lost again to the Germans. And in the summer of 1918, it would be retaken by the Allies.

By 1917, the Allied blockade of German seaports was causing increasing food shortages.
Here, a crowd gathers as a woman serves food from a portable stove in a suburb of Berlin.

—13—

"LAFAYETTE, WE ARE HERE!"— AMERICA JOINS THE FIGHT

The French and British armies were finding it hard to maintain their fighting strength. Their urgent need was for more men, yet months would pass before American troops would arrive in Europe in numbers great enough to make a difference. And now that Russia had been knocked out of the war, the Germans were sending huge numbers of troops to challenge the outnumbered Allies on the Western Front.

The question was: Could the Allies hold out until the Americans arrived in force? In February 1918, after a meeting of the Allied Supreme War Council, the American representative reported: "I doubt if I could make anyone not present at the recent meeting . . . realize the anxiety and fear that pervades the ranks of political and military men here."

The Germans had anxieties and fears of their own. After four punishing wartime winters, the stranglehold of the Allied blockade was causing increasing hardship in Germany and growing demands for peace. Scuffles broke out among people waiting in bread lines. Shortages of food, fuel, and everything else led to strikes and riots in several German cities.

The Reichstag, the German parliament, had passed a Peace Resolution, calling for "a peace of understanding and the permanent reconciliation of peoples without the forcible acquisition of territory." But the German High Command was not prepared to surrender the territories in Belgium, France, and Russia occupied by German armies. To give up those conquered lands, German leaders argued, would be to lose the war.

General Erich Ludendorff believed that Germany could achieve victory on the Western Front by launching one final offensive. With their superior numbers, the Germans could cripple the Allied armies once and for all. But they must attack right away, Ludendorff insisted, before the Americans arrived to tip the balance. It was Germany's one remaining chance to strike a knock-out blow against the Allies.

Ludendorff launched his offensive on the morning of March 21, 1918, against British troops occupying the old Somme battlefield of 1916. By attacking along the Somme, the Germans expected to draw British reserves down from the north, where a second German attack would drive toward the English Channel seaports so crucial to British supply lines.

A heavy fog helped German troops break through British defenses, and by the end of March the Germans had advanced as far as forty miles. But then their offensive sputtered to a halt as infantrymen and horse-drawn artillery became ensnared in the obstacle course of churned-up fields, abandoned trenches, and shattered roads left from the Battle of the Somme.

After two weeks, Ludendorff called off the Somme offensive and shifted to the north, striking near the ruins of Ypres. But the

German reserve troops advance along a road crossing the old Somme battlefield, March 1918.

British lines held, and again Ludendorff called off the attack. So far he had lost 350,000 men. The British had lost almost that many, but they had blocked the German offensive.

Stymied by the British, Ludendorff turned on the French. On May 27, German troops attacked the strategic Chemin des Dames ridge, where the French general Nivelle had launched his disastrous offensive the year before. Moving swiftly, the Germans crossed the Aisne River and advanced as far south as Château-Thierry. After four years, German soldiers were back on the banks of the Marne, which they had first reached in 1914.

By early June, the Germans were within forty miles of Paris, close enough to bombard the French capital with the long-range guns the Allies called Big Berthas. But again the German offensive slowed to a halt in the face of determined Allied resistance. During their advance across the Marne, the Germans had lost another 130,000 men. And some of them had been killed or captured by the newly arrived Americans.

Yeomanettes attached to the U.S. Naval Reserve in San Francisco. They filled secretarial and clerical jobs, freeing men for combat duty.

Even before the United States officially entered the war, American volunteers were fighting alongside the Allies in Europe. Some adventurous young Americans had enlisted in the Canadian or British armies or joined the French Foreign Legion. About two hundred American pilots were serving in the French air force, where they formed the Lafayette Escadrille (Lafayette Squadron), credited with downing 199 German planes. Veterans of this group would transfer their flying skills to the Aviation Section of the U.S. Army Signal Corps, once it arrived in Europe.

Thousands of American volunteers, men and women, were serving in France as ambulance drivers and as nurses and nurses' aides in field hospitals near the frontlines. All together, more than 15,000 women saw overseas service with the American Expeditionary Force and with volunteer organizations such as the American Red Cross. Of these, 120 American nurses died in Europe, and 200 were decorated for bravery.

At home, the U.S. Navy enlisted female clerks as "yeomanettes," who were barred from sea duty but given formal naval rank. And as millions of men left the labor force to enter the armed services, American women, like their counterparts in Europe, went to work in war factories and at other jobs that had been traditionally reserved for men. However, it wasn't until after the war, in 1920, that women in the United States won the right to vote.

America, meanwhile, was mobilizing. When the United States declared war, it had a large and modern navy but a small, poorly equipped army, only the seventeenth largest in the world. Because there weren't enough rifles to go around, many early recruits drilled with broomsticks. The government decided at the outset that the American Expeditionary Force would be made up mostly of draftees. Conscription was introduced in May 1917, and by the war's end, nearly 4 million men were serving with the United States ground forces.

As in Europe, a government-sponsored propaganda campaign in the United States promoted anti-German feelings and enthusiasm for the war effort. Newspapers, books, posters, speakers, and films, such as *The Kaiser: The Beast of Berlin,* helped shape public opinion. Even so, some Americans opposed the war and the draft. Those who protested could be penalized under the 1917 Espionage Act, which made it a crime to interfere with the draft or encourage "disloyal" acts. The Sedition Act, passed a year later, outlawed statements that criticized the government or showed disrespect for the flag. More than 2,000 people were prosecuted under these laws, and some were sentenced to long prison terms.

General John J. Pershing, commander of the American Expeditionary Force, arrived in France in June 1917. On the Fourth of July, one battalion from his First Division paraded past cheering crowds through the streets of Paris. "Lafayette, we are here!" the Americans announced—a tribute to the Marquis de Lafayette, who sailed to America at the age of nineteen and served as a volunteer under George Washington during the American Revolutionary War.

Top: American recruits scale a wall during basic training at Camp Wadsworth, South Carolina.

Bottom: General John J. Pershing, a West Pointer who led the American Expeditionary Force in France.

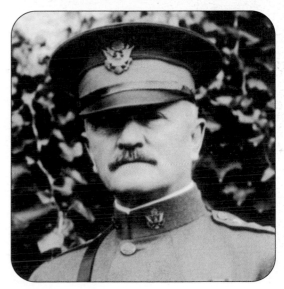

Crowds cheer as American troops arrive in Perth, Scotland, 1918.

By early 1918, American troops were arriving in France at the rate of 120,000 a month. And by summer, well over a million Americans were deployed on the Western Front. Popularly known as "Yanks" or "doughboys" (nicknamed for the shape of the large buttons on their uniforms, which resembled a type of fried bread dough), the long-awaited Americans brought renewed hope to the battle-weary Allies and were welcomed everywhere. Much was expected of them. They would fight at first in small units attached to the French and British armies, and eventually as an independent American army under General Pershing's command.

English author Vera Brittain, then serving as a volunteer nurse in France, remembered watching a large contingent of soldiers pass by one afternoon and wondering where they were from: "They were swinging rapidly toward [the village of] Camiers, and though the sight of soldiers marching was now too familiar to arouse curiosity, an unusual quality of bold vigour in their stride caused me to stare at them with puzzled interest. They looked larger than ordinary men; their tall, straight figures were in vivid contrast to the undersized armies of pale recruits to which we were grown accustomed." As she watched, she heard an excited cry from a group of nurses behind her: "Look! Look! Here are the Americans!"

In their first significant action, on May 28, 1918, 4,000 American troops of the First Division, supported by French artillery, tanks, and air cover, stormed the strategically important village of Cantigny on the Somme, captured the village from the Germans, and fought off a German counterattack. During the three-day battle, two hundred Americans were killed and another two hundred incapacitated by German gas attacks. But the Yanks held Cantigny, and they proved to the Germans that they could fight.

In the months that followed, American troops would play an increasingly important role. Early in June, the U.S. Second and Third Divisions attacked the German bridgehead at the riverside town of Château-Thierry, pushed the enemy back across the Marne, and blocked the way to Paris. "We realized the importance of saving Paris," gunner William Maher of the U.S. artillery said later, "and the Allied army was at stake too."

Five miles to the west of Château-Thierry, a forest called the Belleau Wood had become a German stronghold. A brigade of American Marines attached to the Second Division stormed the stubbornly defended wood, which would change hands six times before the Germans were finally expelled. Early in the battle, as the Marines were digging in, some French troops retreating past

Private Louis Nathan Freedman (sitting), sixteen years old, with two army buddies, photographed in France, 1918.

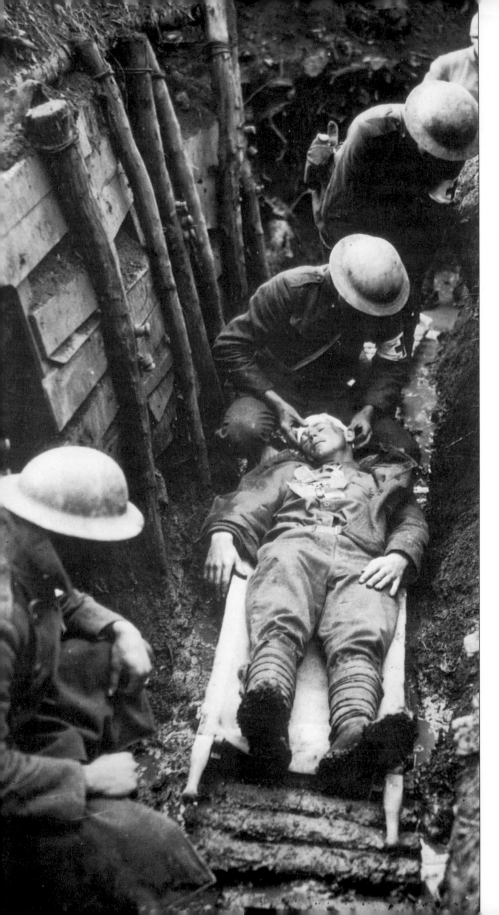

the American position called out to a Marine officer that he and his men had better retreat also. Captain Lloyd Williams answered in words that would become part of Marine lore. "Retreat? Hell, we just got here!"

"We moved into the edge of Belleau Wood, and there facing us from the hill opposite, not more than a few hundred yards away, were the German positions," Marine sergeant Melvin Krulewitch recalled. "We could see the Germans from where we were; we could see the ambulances driving along the ridge to pick up their wounded. We dug foxholes first and then later a trench system. . . .

"The difficulty with Belleau Wood was you never knew where the front was. Little groups of men—Americans, little groups of Germans—got together to fight each other. While we were fighting in one direction all of a sudden without any warning you'd find there were some Germans to the rear of you who had to be mopped up. We had to clean up, mop up, and move ahead. Move ahead with the unyielding determination to enforce our will on the enemy: that was how we moved in Belleau Wood. . . .

"In the rocky crevices and in the little foxholes that the Germans had made—we found the German dead. We found not only the German dead from the day before, but dead from four or five days before, that the enemy hadn't had time to bury. That was Belleau Wood. Fighting from hand to hand: from position to position; not knowing where the next attack would come; but the steady moving forward until we cleared the entire woods."

It took three weeks of bitter fighting and 10,000 American casualties before the Marines gained control of the wood, blocking another German approach to Paris and putting an end to the last major German offensive of the war. The French name for the wood, Bois de Belleau, was later changed to Bois de la Brigade Marine, in honor of the Americans who fought and died there.

Opposite: A wounded marine receives first aid before being sent to the hospital, March 1918.

French civilians sit in the rubble beside the road as American troops pass through St. Baussant during the march to Saint-Mihiel, September 13, 1918.

— 14 —

THE LAST OFFENSIVE
AND THE COLLAPSE OF EMPIRES

Once again, a German offensive had been halted just outside the gates of Paris. Reinforced now by battle-ready American troops, the Allies mounted a massive counterattack. There was little the exhausted Germans could do but order a retreat, and by August 1918 they had been driven back to the Aisne River. To the north, German armies were retreating along the old Somme battlefield, abandoning land they had captured when starting their last-ditch offensive earlier that year.

Until now, American troops had been fighting as part of the French and British armies. In September, General Pershing took command of the U.S. First Army and launched the war's first major independent American offensive. The objective was a large concentration of German troops around the town of Saint-Mihiel, south of Verdun. "The sky over the battlefield, both before and after dawn, aflame with exploding shells, star signals, burning supply dumps and villages, presented a scene at once picturesque and terrible," Pershing wrote. "The exaltation in our minds that here, at last, after seventeen months of effort, an American army was fighting under its own flag was tempered by the realization of the sacrifice of life on both sides."

The Germans were caught by surprise as 200,000 American troops, backed by 48,000 French, attacked in drizzling rain and mist along a twelve-mile front. "American tanks do not surrender as long as one tank is able to go forward," Lieutenant-Colonel George Patton, Jr., instructed his men. The attack was supported by the greatest air assault of the war. Nearly 1,500 planes saw action in the skies above the battlefield, strafing German trenches and dropping bombs on the retreating enemy.

Within forty-eight hours, the Americans had taken Saint-Mihiel, captured 13,000 prisoners, and driven the Germans from positions they had held for four years—"as swift and neat an operation as any in the war," reported the *Manchester Guardian,* a leading British newspaper. It was a victory won at a cost of more than 4,000 American lives.

From Saint-Mihiel, the U.S. Army moved north of Verdun to an area between the Meuse River and the Argonne Forest, where the Americans joined the final Allied offensive of World War I. The Meuse-Argonne campaign would be the war's biggest American battle. Its objective was to capture the critical railroad hub at the city of Sedan, which would break the rail network supporting the German army in France and Belgium.

Fighting against stiff German resistance lasted for six weeks—from September 26 to November 11, 1918. The Meuse River, wide and deep, followed a twisting course between high cliffs, from which German gunners could fire down on the Americans and the French forces on their left flank. The forest itself, ten miles across, was a tangled thicket of trees and thorny underbrush

American doughboys roll toward the Argonne Forest in French Renault six-ton tanks, September 26, 1918.

honeycombed with German tunnels, concrete dugouts, and machine-gun nests that the Germans had spent four years fortifying.

"On arriving at our new positions in the Argonne Forest, we found out that . . . the fighting at this point must have been terrific," recalled Private McGuire, an American artilleryman. "Thousands of trees were splintered, crushed down into the mud, and it made it hard for us to travel. We got our guns into position quickly because the amount of shelling that was done by the Germans had every man of us scared."

Early in the battle, Major Charles Whittlesey of the U.S. Seventy-seventh Division and more than five hundred men, trapped in a ravine behind enemy lines, were surrounded by a much larger force of Germans. For two days, the Americans fought off the enemy troops. On the second day, their food ran out. Then they were hit by an American artillery barrage intended for the Germans.

Private Omer Richards had carried into battle a cage holding eight carrier pigeons, birds trained to carry messages between specific locations. Several birds, dispatched with messages asking for help, had been shot down. By now there was just one bird left—a favorite named Cher Ami, French for "Dear Friend." Richards clipped a message to the pigeon's left leg, giving the Americans' location: "We are along the road parallel to [map reference] 276.4. Our own artillery is dropping a barrage directly on us. For heaven's sake, stop it!"

Cher Ami flew off through a blizzard of enemy bullets and exploding shells. The bird reached his loft, twenty-five miles to the rear, just twenty-five minutes later. He had been shot through the breast and blinded in one eye. But he had delivered the message clipped to his leg, which also had been hit by a bullet and was dangling by a tendon. The shelling was immediately halted.

Nothing else was heard from the beleaguered Americans, who had become known to the world as the Lost Battalion. In an effort to rescue them, two divisions moved out toward the German lines, and as they approached, the Germans withdrew. On October 7, after a five-day siege, the 194 survivors of the Lost Battalion's 554 men climbed out of their ravine and marched back to the American lines.

Cher Ami lost his shattered leg, but army medics carved a small wooden leg for him. The French awarded the doughty little pigeon their Croix de Guerre medal for bravery under fire. And he was sent to the United States to become an army mascot.

Four African American infantry regiments—the U.S. Army was strictly segregated by race—saw heavy fighting during the Meuse-Argonne campaign. Each all-black regiment was equipped by and

served with a French division. The 369th, popularly known as the Harlem Hellfighters, fought with the French at Château-Thierry and Belleau Wood, spending 191 days in combat, longer than any other American unit. Corporal Henry Johnson and Private Needham Roberts became the first Americans to receive the French Croix de Guerre, and when the 369th captured the important village of Sechault, the entire regiment was awarded the Croix de Guerre.

The Meuse-Argonne Offensive was part of a larger Allied offensive taking place all along the Western Front as German armies fell back to the Hindenburg Line—their last line of resistance. Battlefields from which the Allies had been driven earlier in the war were now swiftly overrun. The Germans no longer had the manpower to make up for their losses, while more and more Allied divisions were moving up to the frontlines. This relentless push by British, French, Belgian, and American armies fighting

Top: African American combat troops stand on parade in France, 1918. They were equipped by and fought with the French.

Bottom: Members of the all-black 369th Regiment, the Harlem Hellfighters. The entire regiment was awarded France's Croix de Guerre medal for gallantry in action.

An American machine-gun crew battles in the Argonne Forest.

side by side finally broke the spirit of the German army and ended its willingness to continue a hopeless fight.

On September 28, General Ludendorff informed Kaiser Wilhelm that there was now no prospect of winning the war. The German army had been crippled by a sense of "looming defeat," Ludendorff said, because of "the sheer number of Americans arriving daily at the front." To avert a catastrophe, Ludendorff told the kaiser, Germany must seek an immediate armistice.

Still, the war continued. More than a million American soldiers were now fighting in the Argonne. Despite setbacks and heavy casualties, the Americans finally broke through the German defenses, and by the end of October, they had cleared the forest of enemy troops. "The roads and fields were strewn with dead Germans, horses, masses of artillery, transport, ammunition limbers, helmets, guns and bayonets," Private Rush Young recalled.

Early in November, the U.S. First Division reached the hills overlooking Sedan, then moved aside to allow the French Army the honor of capturing the city, the site of a French defeat in the Franco-Prussian War of 1870.

French, British, and Belgian armies, meanwhile, were assaulting German defenses along the rest of the Western Front. "The morale of the troops has suffered seriously," a German general reported, "and their power of resistance diminishes daily. They surrender in hordes whenever the enemy attacks. . . . Whatever happens we must make peace, before the enemy break through into Germany."

Behind the lines, Germany was on the verge of chaos. At the end of October, German naval crews mutinied, and within a week, revolutionary outbreaks had spread to every big German city. On November 9, the generals, fearing the kind of full-fledged revolution that had occurred in Russia, informed Kaiser Wilhelm that he no longer commanded the confidence of the army. "The Kaiser must abdicate, otherwise we shall have the revolution," he was

German troops surrender to an advancing Allied force as it nears the Hindenburg Line.

For these German prisoners, the war was over.

told. "Your abdication has become necessary to save Germany from civil war."

Wilhelm fled across the Dutch border to take refuge in neutral Holland, where he signed his formal abdication as king of Prussia and German emperor. Germany was declared a republic. In Berlin, a delegation was formed to meet with Allied war leaders and ask for surrender terms.

Germany's partners among the Central Powers had already sued for peace. Bulgaria, deprived of German and Austrian support, was the first to surrender to the Allies, signing an armistice agreement on September 29.

Turkey capitulated a month later, on October 30. In the Middle East, the Turks had suffered a series of defeats by the British, who captured Baghdad in March 1917 and Palestine in September 1918. With Turkey's collapse, the seven-century-old Turkish Ottoman Empire vanished into history.

Austria-Hungary, threatened with a complete breakdown of order as people in the cities starved and rioted, signed an armistice agreement on November 3. The Austrian army had been routed when the Italians, heavily reinforced by British and French divisions, finally went on the offensive. Austrian troops, ragged and hungry, deserted by the thousands. Austria-Hungary would be split up into several smaller nations, putting an end to the Hapsburg Empire.

On November 7, with Berlin and other German cities in turmoil and Kaiser Wilhelm about to abdicate, a German delegation crossed the frontline under a flag of truce to meet with Marshal Ferdinand Foch, commander in chief of the Allied armies, in his railroad carriage in the forest of Compiègne, north of Paris. Germany had not actually surrendered but had asked for an armistice (a cease-fire) to discuss possible peace terms. An armistice would end the fighting but not necessarily the war. In theory, it would have been possible for the Germans to refuse the Allied terms and continue the battle.

The armistice terms presented by Marshal Foch were designed to make sure that the Germans would have no further power to resist. All occupied territories in France and Belgium were to be evacuated immediately, and all territory conquered in eastern Europe since 1914, including lands ceded by Russia at Brest-Litovsk, was to be surrendered. Massive quantities of weapons and other military equipment, including most of the German navy and all German submarines, were to be handed over to the Allies. Allied forces would temporarily occupy a band of German territory along the Rhine River, and Germany would be required to pay reparations, or damages, for the loss and destruction caused by the war. Finally, the Allied blockade of German ports would continue until a peace treaty was signed.

The Germans protested that the terms were too harsh, that the continuing blockade would lead to famine and anarchy in Germany. Foch was unmoved. The Germans had no alternative but to sign.

On November 11, 1918, shortly after five a.m., the two sides signed an armistice agreement that would go into effect at eleven that morning. At two minutes before eleven, as millions of soldiers on the Western Front waited for the hostilities to end, a

Marshal Ferdinand Foch (second from right) stands outside his railroad carriage after signing the armistice agreement.

Canadian soldier, Private George Price, was killed by a German sniper's bullet at the French village of Ville-sur-Haine.

Then it was over. On November 11 at eleven a.m.—the eleventh hour of the eleventh day of the eleventh month—the guns fell silent on the Western Front.

American troops at the front hoist a flag and celebrate after the last shot has been fired, November 11, 1918.

Armistice Day: Thousands of Philadelphians celebrate the end of
the war beneath a replica of the Statue of Liberty on Broad Street.

—❈—15—❈—

LOSING THE PEACE

On the morning of November 11, 1918, Major Keith Officer, an Australian, was watching the minutes go around on his large, old-fashioned hunting watch as he waited for the cease-fire to begin. "Nearby there was a German machine gun unit giving our troops a lot of trouble," he remembered. "They kept on firing until practically 11 o'clock. At precisely 11 o'clock an officer stepped out of their position, stood up, lifted his helmet and bowed to the British troops. He then fell in all his men in the front of the trench and marched them off. I always thought that this was a wonderful display of confidence in British chivalry, because the temptation to fire on them must have been very great."

"The armistice came, the day we dreamed of," recalled British sergeant-major Richard Tobin. "The guns stopped, the fighting stopped. Four years of noise and bangs ended in silence. The killings had stopped.

American troops returning home from France sail into New York Harbor.

"We were stunned. I had been out since 1914. I should have been happy. I was sad. I thought of the slaughter, the hardships, the waste and the friends I had lost."

News of the armistice spread swiftly around the world. In every Allied capital, and cities all over the world, exuberant crowds poured into the streets, cheering and hugging soldiers in uniform, singing, dancing, and rejoicing. "We danced on the buses, we danced on the lorries [trucks], we danced on the pavement, we shouted, we sang," wrote Sir Evelyn Wrendy, recalling Armistice Day in London. "We cheered and cheered again and again, while church bells rang out in a peal of jubilation."

Those who had lost loved ones in the war, or had been crippled or maimed, could not so easily put sorrowful memories aside. Robert Graves, badly wounded in the Battle of the Somme, had been posted back to England. He was training cadets at a camp in North Wales when the armistice was announced. He had just learned of the deaths in battle of two close friends. And two months earlier, his wife's brother had been killed in France.

"Armistice night hysteria did not touch our camp much, though some of the Canadians stationed there went down to [the town of] Rhyl to celebrate in true overseas style," Graves wrote. "The news sent me out walking alone . . . cursing and sobbing and thinking of the dead."

The cost of World War I in human lives is difficult to estimate with accuracy and is impossible to imagine. About 65 million men were mobilized to fight. During four years of slaughter, more than half of those men became casualties: 8.5 million killed, 21 million wounded, nearly 8 million missing in action or taken prisoner. In addition, an estimated 10 million civilians perished of war-related famine and disease.

Among the combatant nations in Europe, there was scarcely a family that had not lost a son, a brother, or a father. Some families lost every male member, leaving behind widows and orphans and shattered dreams. After the war, people would speak of a "lost generation." And among those who survived, hundreds of thousands had lost an arm or a leg or had been hideously deformed by battle wounds.

Today, the entire length of the Western Front is marked by hundreds of graveyards and memorials to the soldiers who lost their lives fighting there. The Meuse-Argonne American Cemetery holds the graves of 14,246 war dead, most of whom fell during the U.S. Army's Meuse-Argonne offensive in the autumn of 1918. The graves are still visited, often by the grandchildren and great-grandchildren of the men buried there; scattered among the long rows of headstones, bouquets of fresh flowers and cards of remembrance pay tribute to those who gave their lives nearly a century ago.

Along with the toll of human lives, entire towns and villages had been wiped off the map, to be remembered, if at all, by means

Left behind: The Meuse-Argonne American Cemetery in 2008, ninety years after the war ended.

of small stone monuments that resemble graveyard headstones. Vast expanses of fertile farmland had been blasted and burned into a pockmarked wasteland. The European economy had been devastated. And war had left a bitter legacy of rage and a desire for revenge. After four years of misery and suffering, it is little wonder that people everywhere in Europe hoped and prayed—and to some extent believed—that this would be "the war to end all wars."

In January 1919, Allied statesmen met near Paris to discuss a final peace settlement. Dozens of nations were invited to attend, but in the end the conference was dominated by three men: French premier Georges Clemenceau, British prime minister David Lloyd George, and American president Woodrow Wilson. Clemenceau, with the wholehearted support of his countrymen, was determined to make sure that Germany would never again be powerful enough to threaten the peace of Europe. In the French view, everything possible had to be done to keep Germany weak and divided.

Lloyd George also wanted Germany disarmed, but he was more cautious than Clemenceau. Before the war, Germany had been Britain's largest trading partner. Germany must be punished, Lloyd George agreed, but not so severely that the country would be left destitute or vulnerable to the spread of communism from Russia.

Wilson's chief concern was his idealistic scheme for a world organization to prevent future wars. His vision of a new Europe included a League of Nations, in which "great and small states alike" would settle their differences peacefully instead of going to war.

Disagreements among Wilson, Lloyd George, and Clemenceau erupted into angry arguments. Negotiations almost broke down several times before a final agreement was reached in June 1919. The result, a compromise, imposed harsh peace terms on a defeated Germany.

Allied leaders at the Versailles peace conference (left to right): British prime minister David Lloyd George, Italian prime minister Vittorio Orlando, French prime minister Georges Clemenceau, and U.S. president Woodrow Wilson. Orlando was frequently left on the sidelines when critical negotiations took place among the other three.

The treaty stated that Germany was solely and entirely responsible for the war. The Germans were required to disarm, to surrender their overseas colonies, and to pay massive reparations for the losses suffered by the Allies. The provinces of Alsace and Lorraine were to be returned to France. Germany would also lose large chunks of territory to Belgium and other neighboring states, to newly independent Poland, and to other newborn nations created by Allied statesmen as they redrew the map of Europe. The collapsed empires of Germany, Austria-Hungary, and Russia were replaced by a patchwork of smaller nations with their own armies, alliances, and jealousies.

The Allies also redrew the map of the Middle East. With the breakup of the Ottoman Empire and the release of Arab lands from Turkish rule, that oil-rich region was divided into spheres of British and French influence. France took control of Lebanon and Syria. Britain administered Palestine, opening it to immigration by European Jews, and created a new puppet kingdom called Iraq (formerly Mesopotamia), planting the seeds for future generations of discord and strife.

Victorious British troops march into Baghdad, March 11, 1917. With the defeat of the Turkish Ottoman Empire, Britain created a new puppet kingdom called Iraq, with Baghdad as its capital.

Germany and its former allies had not been allowed to take part in the negotiations. At first the Germans refused to sign the peace agreement. But they had little choice. They had already turned over most of their arms and warships to the Allies. Germany was incapable now of defending itself, and the continuing Allied blockade of German ports was causing increasing misery. When the Allies threatened to invade, the Germans relented.

The treaty formally ending World War I was signed by representatives of the Allied powers and the German government in the Hall of Mirrors of the Palace of Versailles near Paris on June 28, 1919. Forty-eight years earlier, following Germany's victory in the Franco-Prussian War, the now-defunct German Empire had been proclaimed in the same ornate hall.

The Treaty of Versailles was a compromise that pleased no one. French premier Clemenceau had failed to achieve all the demands of the French people, who complained that the peace terms were too lenient and that Germany should have been partitioned into smaller, weaker states. "This is not peace," declared French field marshal Ferdinand Foch. "It is an armistice for twenty years."

Crowded into the ornate Hall of Mirrors of the Palace of Versailles, dignitaries and government officials observe the formal signing of the peace treaty, June 28, 1919.

EUROPE AFTER THE WAR

British prime minister Lloyd George worried that certain treaty terms would prove "a constant source of irritation," stirring up resentment among the Germans. The sooner the question of reparations could be resolved, he said, the better. And he criticized the transfer of territory populated by large numbers of Germans "from German rule to the rule of other nations," since those people would soon be "clamoring for reunion with their native land." When the treaty was finally approved in 1919, Lloyd George gloomily predicted, "We shall have to fight another war all over again in twenty-five years." Foch's twenty-year prophecy was more accurate: Europe went to war again in September 1939.

Today, most historians agree that the Treaty of Versailles helped set the stage for World War II. They consider the First and Second World Wars part of the same struggle. "The Second World War was the continuation of the First," writes historian John Keegan, "and indeed [World War II] is inexplicable except in terms of the rancor and instabilities left by the earlier conflict."

The peace terms caused lingering resentments in Germany. Germans were embittered by the way so many German speakers were placed under the rule of other countries. The demands for huge reparations—far more than could ever be paid—were seen as unjust. So was the fact that Germany was given no say in the treaty terms. What rankled most was the treaty's humiliating "war guilt" clause, placing the blame entirely at Germany's feet. Germans continued to believe that the war had been forced upon them by their enemies.

The Allies had chosen to deal with officials of Germany's newly formed Weimar Republic, leaving the German army uninvolved. The army now protested that it had never actually surrendered but had simply agreed to a cease-fire, and at the time of the armistice was still in possession of vast conquered territories. Former military leaders and their supporters sought to blame Germany's defeat on cowardly and traitorous liberal politicians, rather than on the exhaustion of the German war machine. The army, they claimed, had been "stabbed in the back."

President Wilson was disappointed in his hope that the League of Nations would preserve world peace. Established by the Treaty of Versailles in 1919, the League was beset with problems from the beginning. Germany was accepted as a member in 1926 and Russia joined in 1934, but ironically, even though Wilson was awarded the Nobel Peace Prize for 1919, the United States refused to join the international organization.

Once the war was over, many Americans felt that the country's intervention in Europe had been a mistake, never to be repeated. Wilson traveled the United States, trying to win support for both the treaty and the League. But many senators were opposed to the treaty as written, and American isolationists wanted to keep the United States out of world affairs. Despite Wilson's efforts, Congress failed to ratify the Treaty of Versailles. As a result, the United States, which had suddenly become the world's most powerful country, never became a member of the League of Nations.

The League had some success in humanitarian work and in settling minor disputes. But it never enjoyed the support it needed to achieve universal disarmament and prevent another war. Italy, Japan, and eventually Germany withdrew in the face of League criticism, and other nations increasingly ignored the organization's decisions. The League's success depended on the willingness of governments to cooperate. But the victorious Allies and the newly formed national states in Europe showed little confidence in the League. Instead, they preferred to rely on their own armed strength.

The defeated countries had been required to disarm. This, the victors argued, would encourage "a general limitation of the armaments of all nations." That never happened. When other nations failed to limit their own forces, Germany denounced the

arms restrictions that had been imposed upon it and began to rearm in earnest.

Many Germans were still bitter about the terms of the Treaty of Versailles. The Allies' insistence that Germany pay billions in war reparations was a source of festering resentment. And when Germany was caught up in the worldwide depression of the early 1930s, Germans were ready to blame the economic disaster that had overwhelmed them on the treaty's demands. A large part of the electorate turned to the Nazi party and its leader, Adolf Hitler, who condemned the peace treaty and vowed to regain Germany's lost territories and restore its military might.

Left: A poster for the 1933 election in Germany during the worldwide economic depression. The words read "Against Hunger and Despair! Vote HITLER!"

Right: Adolf Hitler with Nazi officials at the 1936 Olympic Games in Berlin.

Overleaf: German troops gather on the border with Poland, awaiting the Führer's order to invade.

In 1936, Hitler violated the terms of the Treaty of Versailles by sending troops into the demilitarized German Rhineland. France and Britain took no action to stop him. Other treaty violations followed as the Nazi government annexed Austria, then the Sudetenland region of Czechoslovakia, where many ethnic Germans lived, and finally the rest of Czechoslovakia. Still, the World War I Allies were hesitant to act. Haunted by the immense sacrifices and dreadful memories of World War I, the French and British people were reluctant ever to endure such a bloodletting again. Instead of resisting Nazi Germany's demands, France and Britain followed a policy of appeasement; by giving in to Hitler's lesser demands, they hoped to avoid greater demands in the future. In this way, they allowed Germany to recover its military might.

In September 1939, Hitler invaded Poland, setting loose the Second World War twenty years after Germany's crushing defeat in the First.

Once again, Europe was armed to the teeth.

A night attack with phosphorus bombs
near Gondrecour, France, August 1918.

NOTES

The following notes refer to the sources of quoted material. Each citation includes the first and last words of the quotation and the source. Unless otherwise noted, all references are to works cited in the Selected Bibliography.

Abbreviations used:
Arthur: Max Arthur, *Forgotten Voices of the Great War*
Fussell: Paul Fussell, *The Great War and Modern Memory*
Gilbert: Martin Gilbert, *The First World War: A Complete History*
Graves: Robert Graves, *Good-bye to All That*
Howard: Michael Howard, *The First World War: A Very Short Introduction*
Keegan: John Keegan, *The First World War*
Lewis: Jon E. Lewis, *The Mammoth Book of Eyewitness World War I*
Meyer: G. J. Meyer, *A World Undone: The Story of the Great War 1914 to 1918*
Palmer: Svetlana Palmer and Sarah Wallis, *Intimate Voices from the First World War*
Ross: Stewart Ross, *Causes and Consequences of World War I*
Strachan: Hew Strachan, *The First World War: A New Illustrated History*
Tuchman: Barbara Tuchman, *The Guns of August*

1: MURDER IN SARAJEVO

Page

2   "Death to the tyrant": Lewis, p. 10
     "he only . . . ideals": Meyer, p. 17
3   "So you . . . bombs": Gilbert, p. 16
4   "For heaven's . . . It's nothing": Meyer, p. 8
5   "Greater Serbia": Keegan, p. 50
7   "must be . . . Balkans": Keegan, p. 51
     "The Serbs . . . soon": Gilbert, p. 18
     "The tragedy . . . complications": Gilbert, p. 18

2: ARMED TO THE TEETH

10   "The world . . . dawning": Meyer, p. 11
13   "The accelerating arms race . . . seeks to avert": Keegan, p. 17
     "final and . . . Serbia": Strachan, p. 10

13–14 "Windows . . . started": Strachan, p. 20
14   "and that then . . . prevented": Keegan, p. 63
     "To try . . . too far": Gilbert, p. 26
     "Your very . . . with you": Meyer, p. 72
15   "Think of . . . death": Meyer, p. 76
     "[German] mobilization . . . Austria-Hungary": Keegan, p. 66
     "Mobilization . . . war": Keegan, p. 66
     "I cannot . . . world": Gilbert, p. 30
16   "In that case . . . want to": Gilbert, p. 30

3: TO BERLIN! TO PARIS!

22   "before the leaves . . . trees": Tuchman, p. 119
     "To Berlin!": Meyer, p. 73
22–23 "In the first . . . three months": Arthur, p. 11
24–25 "I'd never . . . was there": Arthur, p. 67
25   "All Highest War Lord": Jan Rüger, *The*

Great Naval Game: Britain and Germany in the Age of Empire (Cambridge: Cambridge University Press, 2007), p. 189
"A fateful . . . army": Keegan, p. 71
"That is . . . struggle": Lewis, p. 24
27   "I could . . . Embassy": Lewis, p. 16
       "However . . . Germans": Meyer, p. 501
27–29 "Our march . . . nation": Lewis, p. 24
29   "At six . . . *À bientôt!*": Keegan, p. 72
       "discovered . . . war": Meyer, p. 74
       "'Patriots' . . . citizens": Lewis, pp. 25–27

4: "The Most Terrible August
   in the History of the World"
31–32 "came on line . . . them back": Tuchman, p. 174
32   "the whole village . . . wall": Tuchman, p. 174
       "Our advance . . . consequences": Tuchman, p. 174
       "the Oxford of Belgium": Keegan, p. 82
       "Snipers! Snipers!": Keegan, p. 83
33   "rape of Belgium": Keegan, p. 82
34   "aroused . . . Germany": Tuchman, p. 322
35   "The French . . . field": Keegan, p. 96; quoted from Sewell Tyng, *The Campaign of the Marne* (New York: Longmans, Green, 1935), p. 108
       "It is clear . . . gunfire": Meyer, p. 142
       "The most . . . world": Meyer, p. 162
36   "soon began . . . knees": Keegan, p. 107
       "Our soldiers . . . march": Keegan, p. 201
37   "Attack . . . the other": Tuchman, p. 435
       "The heat . . . intolerable": Meyer, p. 208
39   "Miracle of the Marne": Tuchman, p. 436
       "That men . . . academy": Tuchman, p. 436

5: Stalemate
42   "Every day . . . like this": Palmer, pp. 33–34
45   "The [czar] . . . disaster": Gilbert, p. 49
       "Shackled to a corpse": Strachan, p. 31
48   "I think . . . Christmas": Gilbert, p. 118
49   "I issued . . . must cease": Gilbert, p. 119

6: The Technology of Death and Destruction
52   "creeping barrage": Howard, p. 39
54–55 "When the first . . . infantry": Meyer, p. 586
57   "quite 200 . . . suffering": Keegan, p. 199
60   "We literally . . . weeks": Meyer, p. 411

7: Life and Death in the Trenches
63   "We went . . . be like": Graves, p. 95
65–66 "One night . . . later": Arthur, pp. 45–46
66   "were sticky . . . next room": Graves, p. 98
66–67 "There are . . . they fall": Strachan, p. 159
67–68 "scores of men . . . thousands": Gilbert, p. 219
68   "In this sunshine . . . face": quoted in Fussell, p. 164
69   "a hair-raising . . . haze": Strachan, p. 163

8: Over the Top
73   "Then, it was . . . shells": Arthur, p. 186
75–76 "It was foggy . . . weren't hit": Arthur, pp. 76–77
76   "could only . . . sleepers": Gilbert, p. 133
       "I was wounded . . . could have": Arthur, p. 76
76–77 "We relieved . . . properly": Lewis, p. 112
77–78 "I'd never . . . we look": Arthur, pp. 90–91
79   "Coming back . . . front": Arthur, p. 101
       "melting like snow": Palmer, p. 109
80   "so weakened . . . future": Meyer, p. 363
80–81 "All the villagers . . . around them": Palmer, p. 107

9: The Battle of Verdun
85   "No line . . . safe": Keegan, p. 279
86   "The strain . . . reached": Keegan, p. 278
       "compel the French . . . death": Keegan, p. 278
       "Operation Judgment": Keegan, p. 278
87   "The commanding . . . to do": Keegan, p. 281
       "Retake . . . pass": Gilbert, p. 232
88   "the last . . . them": Keegan, p. 283
89–90 "It's hell . . . help them": Lewis, pp. 208–9

10: THE BATTLE OF THE SOMME

94   "I feel . . . so thorough": Fussell, p. 29
      "At 7:30 . . . objective": Strachan, p. 188
95   "I see . . . like this": Fussell, pp. 29–30
96   "When the leading . . . death": Lewis,
      p. 214
97   "When we started . . . them": Meyer, p. 446
98   "an amazing . . . sides": Lewis, p. 215
98–99 "one summer . . . going on": Arthur, p. 166
101   "Humanity is . . . men are mad": Gilbert,
      p. 250

11: THE WAR AT SEA

105   "Travelers . . . risk": Gilbert, p. 156
106–7 "There was . . . bo-at": Lewis, pp. 93–96
107   "The English . . . operations": Gilbert, p. 157
108   "turnip winter": Keegan, p. 318
109   "hunger-blockade": Gilbert, p. 128
      "There can be . . . ground": Meyer, p. 367
110   "Fear . . . success": Keegan, p. 352
111   "He kept us out of war": Meyer, p. 474
112   "Zimmermann telegram": Keegan, p. 351
113   "war against all nations": Keegan, p. 352
      "The world . . . democracy": Gilbert, p. 317

12: MUTINY, REVOLUTION, AND THE COLLAPSE OF ARMIES

116   "rupture": Keegan, p. 327
      "the mutinies of 1917": Keegan, p. 329
117   "I set . . . soldiers": Gilbert, p. 334
      "acts of collective indiscipline": Keegan,
      p. 329
120   "the most . . . war": Keegan, p. 355
122   "The ground . . . them up": Keegan, p. 361
123   "The enemy . . . results": Keegan, p. 366
123–24 "Up the road . . . help them": Keegan,
      p. 363
124   "my worst . . . remained": Keegan, p. 364

13: "LAFAYETTE, WE ARE HERE!" —AMERICA JOINS THE FIGHT

127   "I doubt . . . here": Howard, p. 96
128   "a peace . . . territory": Howard, p. 97

130   "yeomanettes": Meyer, p. 669
131   "Lafayette, we are here!": *The New
      Dictionary of Cultural Literacy,* 3rd ed.,
      by E. D. Hirsch Jr., Joseph F. Kett, and
      James Trefil (New York: Houghton
      Mifflin, 2002); www.bartleby.
      com/59/11/lafayetteman.html
133   "They were . . . Americans": Gilbert, p. 414
      "We realized . . . too": Arthur, p. 291
134   "Retreat . . . got here": Keegan, p. 407
134–35 "We moved . . . entire woods": Arthur,
      pp. 288–89

14: THE LAST OFFENSIVE AND THE COLLAPSE OF EMPIRES

137–38 "The sky . . . sides": Lewis, p. 421
138   "American tanks . . . forward": Gilbert,
      p. 458
      "as swift . . . war": Gilbert, p. 459
139   "On arriving . . . scared": Arthur, p. 304
140   "We are . . . stop it": Wikipedia, "Cher
      Ami"
142   "looming defeat . . . armistice": Keegan,
      p. 411
      "The roads . . . bayonets": Gilbert, p. 490
143   "The morale . . . Germany": Howard,
      p. 110
      "The Kaiser . . . war": Keegan, p. 417

15: LOSING THE PEACE

149   "Nearby . . . very great": Arthur,
      pp. 209–11
149–50 "The armistice . . . had lost": Arthur, p. 313
150   "We danced . . . jubilation": Ross, p. 67
151   "Armistice night . . . dead": Graves,
      pp. 277–78
      "lost generation": Keegan, p. 423
152   "the war to end all wars": Keegan, p. 9
153   "great and small states alike": Howard,
      p. 123
155   "This is not . . . years": Ruth Henig,
      Versailles and After: 1931–1933, 2nd ed.
      (London: Routledge, 1995), p. 52

157 "a constant source of irritation": Gilbert, p. 513

"from German . . . native land": Gilbert, p. 513

"We shall . . . years": Ross, p. 62

"The Second . . . conflict": Keegan, p. 423

"war guilt": Gilbert, p. 518

158 "stabbed in the back": Meyer, p. 711

"a general . . . nations": Howard, p. 115

British troops advance at dusk.

Selected Bibliography

The First World War has fascinated, horrified, and puzzled every generation since then and inspired a vast literature of histories, memoirs, novels, poems, films, and plays. *Journey's End,* playwright R. C. Sherriff's powerful World War I drama, was first staged in London in 1928. I saw the Broadway revival in 2007. The play reminded me that World War I was my father's war, and as I left the theater, I was determined to write this book.

Among many recent histories, I am particularly indebted to John Keegan's *The First World War* (New York: Alfred Knopf, 1999); Martin Gilbert's *The First World War: A Complete History* (New York: Henry Holt, 1994); G. J. Meyer's *A World Undone: The Story of the Great War 1914 to 1918* (New York: Delacorte, 2006); and Hew Strachan's *The First World War: A New Illustrated History* (London: Simon & Schuster, 2003). Michael Howard's *The First World War: A Very Short Introduction* (New York: Oxford University Press, 2002) offers a remarkably concise and solid account of the war.

Barbara W. Tuchman's *The Guns of August* (New York: Macmillan, 1962) is a Pulitzer Prize–winning account of the war's outbreak. Paul Fussell's *The Great War and Modern Memory* (New York: Oxford University Press, 1975 and 2000), winner of the National Book Award, is a landmark cultural study of how World War I and the literature of the war changed our view of the world.

Robert Graves's *Good-bye to All That* (New York: Anchor Books, 1998; first published in 1929) is probably the most widely read English-language memoir of the war. Ernst Jünger's *Storm of Steel,* translated by Michael Hofmann (New York: Penguin Classics, 2004; first published in 1920), is a widely admired memoir by a former German soldier. Compilations of first-hand accounts from interviews, memoirs, journals, and letters include *Forgotten Voices of the Great War,* edited by Max Arthur in association with London's Imperial War Museum (London: Ebury Press, 2002); *Intimate Voices from the First World War,* edited by Svetlana Palmer and Sarah Wallis (New York: William Morrow, 2004); and *The Mammoth Book of Eyewitness World War I,* edited by Jon E. Lewis (New York: Carroll & Graff, 2002).

Susan Sontag's *Regarding the Pain of Others* (New York: Farrar, Straus and Giroux, 2003) and Barbara Ehrenreich's *Blood Rites: Origins and History of the Passions of War* (New York: Metropolitan Books, 1997) offer wide-ranging discussions of the nature of war in general.

Classic World War I novels include Erich Maria Remarque's *All Quiet on the Western Front,* translated from the German by A. W. Wheen (New York: Little, Brown, 1929); Ernest Hemingway's *A Farewell to Arms* (New York: Charles Scribner's Sons, 1929); and more recently, Pat Barker's *Regeneration* (New York: Dutton, 1992), the first novel in Barker's World War I trilogy, which also includes *The Eye in the Door* (1994) and *The Ghost Road* (1995).

Poetry collections include *The Penguin Book of First World War Poetry,* edited by George Walter (New York: Penguin Books, 2006); and *First World War Poems,* edited by Andrew Motion (London: Faber & Faber, 2003).

Noteworthy World War I films include *All Quiet on the Western Front* (1930), based on the Erich Maria Remarque novel; *La Grande Illusion* (1937), in French with English subtitles; and *Paths of Glory* (1957).

World War I histories for young readers include Walter Dean Myers and Bill Miles's *The Harlem Hellfighters: When Pride Met Courage* (New York: Armistad Press, 2005); Simon Adams's *Eyewitness World War I* (New York: DK Publishing, 2007); and Stewart Ross's *Causes and Consequences of World War I* (Austin, Tex.: Raintree Steck-Vaughn, 1998). Among noteworthy novels for young readers are Iain Lawrence's *Lord of the Nutcracker Men* (New York: Delacorte, 2001) and Michael Morpurgo's *Private Peaceful* (New York: Scholastic, 2004). *War and the Pity of War,* edited by Neil Philip and illustrated by Michael McCurdy (New York: Clarion Books, 1998), is a young reader's anthology of war poems spanning the centuries.

Virtually every topic, theme, and personality discussed in this book is represented by one or more corresponding websites, which can be accessed through search engines such as Google. A good place to start would be www.firstworldwar.com.

ACKNOWLEDGMENTS

My thanks to Nagali Henry and Charlene Fanget, Office of Tourism, Verdun; Laura Clouting and Alan S. Wakefield, Imperial War Muscum, London; Gina Marchetti, who persuaded me to begin my research at the Imperial War Museum; and to John Briggs, Evans Chan, George Chiang, Jim Giblin, Regina Griffin, Bella Halsted, and George and Carol Hutchinson, who supplied research materials, suggested leads, and offered encouragement. I am grateful to Donna Brook and Bob Hershon, who read and commented on the manuscript, to Renée Cafiero for her meticulous copyediting, and as always, to my editor, Dinah Stevenson, who is both wise and kind.

PICTURE CREDITS

A solitary American soldier looks at a
ruined church on the crest of Montfaucon,
France, after the town was captured.

Index

Page numbers in **bold** type refer to photos and their captions.